Melanie Kos-Paula

My Husband
My Lord
My All

old things have passed away,
behold, all things have become new

(from my diary)

MINISTRYHOUSE
p u b l i c a t i o n s
www.ministryhouse.com

My Husband
My Lord
My All

old things have passed away,
behold, all things have become new

By Melanie Kos-Paula

MinistryHouse Publications
Po. Bos 233
1100 AA   Diemen
The Netherlands

www.ministryhouse.nl

Translated by Melanie Kos-Paula
Coverdesign: John H. Olsen
Picture back cover by: Gijsbert Kos

All rights reserved 2006 / 2007©
Royal Library Catalog Card Number: 020-14249
International Standard Book Number-13: 978-90-77607-28-2
NUR 707

1234567BP87654321
Published in the Netherlands

It is to be respected that Melanie writes so openheartedly about the things she went through. She takes the reader through her experiences of pain, sorrow and doubt, but also guides them to her world of victory. I am convinced that she is doing many people a great favor with the publication of this book.

Highly recommended!

S.L. Hofwijks, pastor Maranatha Ministries

Very impressive! Surely your life experience will be an encouragement to many who are also going through the deep valleys of life. It has been an encouragement to me also, to read how close God is to us, men.

John Olsen, Director Ministryhouse Publishing

Beautifully and candidly written. My compliments!

Selena Bouman, reader

Melanie Kos-Paula

My Husband
My Lord
My All

old things have passed away,
behold, all things have become new

(from my diary)

MINISTRYHOUSE
p u b l i c a t i o n s
www.ministryhouse.com

The LORD is good to those whose hope is in him,
to the one who seeks him;
it is good to wait quietly
for the salvation of the LORD.
It is good for a man to bear the yoke
while he is young.

Let him sit alone in silence,
for the LORD has laid it on him.
Let him bury his face in the dust—
there may yet be hope.
Let him offer his cheek to one who would strike him,
and let him be filled with disgrace.

For men are not cast off
by the Lord forever.
Though he brings grief, he will show compassion,
so great is his unfailing love.
For he does not willingly bring affliction
or grief to the children of men.

I called on your name, O LORD,
from the depths of the pit.
You heard my plea: "Do not close your ears
to my cry for relief."
You came near when I called you,
and you said, "Do not fear."
(Lamentations 3:25-33, 55-57)

Words of thanks

.

I want to thank everyone who helped and supported me in making this book a reality. I especially want to give a special thanks to the three people who have worked with me on this book as if it were their very own project: my best friend Yunette Aniceta, my dear friend and ex- team leader Francine van Ballegooy, and my father Alejandro Felipe (Jandie) Paula.

God bless you richly!

I dedicate this book to:

■

My dear husband Richard Kos. I never thought that marriage could be so fulfilling! I thank the Lord for his grace that has brought you into my life! I pray that God will continue watching over our marriage. I love you, dushi!

My parents, Jandie and Monica Paula. You have been my help and stay during the tough periods of my life. Thank you for always being there! Never forget how much I love you.

Melanie

Foreword

■

My Husband, My Lord, My All is based on fragments from my diary which I kept from the age of 18 to 33. The book describes the transition of an insecure young girl to a married woman, a marriage in which my husband meant everything to me. Yet, shortly after praying and asking God to make my life useful for His Kingdom and His purposes, a series of unexpected situations made me lose everything that was dear to me, but the difficult and painful experiences I went through eventually led me to get to know the Lord as my True Husband. He became everything to me. It was also in this time that I went through a great spiritual awakening and growth that drew me closer to God and my relationship with Him greatly intensified. A milestone here was my first encounter with the Holy Spirit which was a first step in developing a close, trusting relationship with God. Some of the insights I received from the Holy Spirit are extensively described in this work.

As I matured and life experiences became tougher both the style and depth of my diary entries changed and became more like 'conversations with God'. I learned to turn directly to Him in my writings, especially during difficult times in my life.

The book shows how God literally walked me through an

extremely moving journey from self-insight to forgiveness and finally to complete emotional healing and restoration. You, the reader can see how I allowed the Lord to guide me, build me up and encourage me through verses from the Bible in practically every situation I went through. I looked up some of these verses for you and put them between brackets throughout the book. In doing so I want to encourage you to dig into God's word, the Bible, for yourself and draw from the rich promises He has made, also to you, to help you stand up against the difficulties of life.

On three different occasions in my life I was confirmed that God would use me to bring the gospel of Jesus to others. I am convinced for some time now that this is best achieved by sharing my experiences with others, of what God has meant to me in the most crucial moments of my life. For this reason I'm very grateful that you now have this book in your hands, thus allowing that which I believe that God desires of me to take place.

In December, 2002 I suddenly stopped writing in my diary. It was as if God said: These are all the notes you need in order to be able to write your book. The rest will come of its own accord. So, my story does not end in December 2002. On the contrary, it was only after this time that I was able to reap the fruits of my emotional restoration and truly make a new start with my life. My main goal in writing this book is not to let you share in my pain and blessings. No, my greatest desire is for you to see the greatness and faithfulness of God throughout my life and to realize that He wants to be a reality in your life as well.

My story takes place alternately on my birth island Curaçao and in Holland. Throughout the book it is very clear how experiences of my young years influenced my later life, thus showing that events from the past, present and future are all interwoven.

I hardly mention my parents, who live in Curaçao, in this book. Yet, during this whole process they supported and carried me through in a very special way. They shared my deepest valleys, mainly in the most bitter period of my life from October 1999 to November 2000. On the other hand they were also there to experience my recurring moments of spiritual awakening that grew deeper with time. I therefore want to give them special attention here in my foreword for all that they have meant to me. I also wish to thank all my friends who in one way or another have contributed to me being the person I am today.

About the writing style

My Husband, My Lord, My All is written for the most part in chronological order. Now and then there are flashbacks that connect back to things that happened at a certain moment. Up to Sunday, December 15, 2002 entries are taken directly form my diary and printed in italics. The date on which they were written is found at the top left hand corner of the text. There are also some texts in italics where no specific dates are mentioned. The reason for this is that sometimes several events that were similar in nature have been placed under one heading, so as to benefit the readability of the work.

Some notes from my diary are written in narrative form. I chose for this variation in style to avoid making this book seem like simply a record of random experiences on several days of my life. The intermediate parts written in narrative form function as a 'bridge' and are meant to bind the story together. Some of the narration is supplemented with my own thoughts, feelings and experiences, worded from the point of view of someone who has become richer by her experiences and looks back and reflects on her past. From December 15, 2002, the work is solely written in the narrative form, naturally, because of lack of original diary notes.

Finally I want to mention that all the names in this book, except those of myself and my husband, are fictitious. With regard to the person "Carl" I want to say that it is not at all my intention to hurt or belittle him with this work.

Yet, it is impossible to show the greatness of my God without writing and being honest about the very difficult and painful experiences I went through during this time. All, of course recounted from my own personal experience and perspective. I've made a conscious effort to omit those experiences that were painful but do not necessarily add to the quality of this work. I trust that the choices I made will make this work a lively and captivating whole which you will read with pleasure and interest.

My Husband, My Lord, My All concludes with an invitation to you, the reader, to also entrust your life to the Lord so that you can experience His hand upon your life. I pray that My Husband, My Lord, My All will be an encouragement to you and that you will accept it as a willing hand from God to let you know that He wants to share His great love with you in the good as well as in the bad times of your life.

God bless you!
Melanie Kos-Paula

Contents

∎

Introduction

■

Wednesday, October 06, 1999
Carl left me on September 16, 1999 after we had been
married for four years. He suddenly walked out of my life
because he thinks we've grown apart. He has other interests,
that's what he said to me, while I was mainly interested in
occupying myself with things of the Lord during these past
six months. I yelled at him for answers that never came. All
this started after that one conversation we had ... As he spoke
I felt threatened and my first thought was: "He doesn't want
to be with me anymore". I was hurt and I screamed at him
in desperation and said: "What's the matter, did you meet
some woman somewhere that you would like to go out and
have a good time with? Are you leaving me, is that what it
is? To this last question he answered: "I don't know". My
world crumbled, because to me his answer meant: "Yes, I
am leaving you."
In tears he said to me that I once meant everything to him
and that he had loved me very much, but that he now felt
totally empty inside. Even the last spark of love that he still
had for me in his heart had been quenched, from one day to
another. He says that he has given me all of himself in the
years since he knew me and now feels that he has nothing
left to give ... Carl has been away now for almost four weeks

21

and has moved in with his mother.

Ten days later he came by the apartment to tell me that he was definitely not returning home to me. I broke down in desperation and pain. Since then Carl's heart and spirit are completely closed to me. When I try to touch him I realize how deep his pain is. Physically he is completely distant from me. His facial expression shows me that I mean nothing to him anymore. There are days when I see other expressions, though, but I cannot exactly place them. Maybe he's thinking: "How could we have let this happen?" Or: "Why don't you just forget about this whole thing? Please, just understand that I have nothing more to offer you and that I don't have any feelings for you anymore". I see that he has not been wearing his wedding ring since a few days now. This hurts me so much. I am asking the Lord for faith that moves mountains, but the enemy keeps pointing out to me everything that is going wrong: "See, for him it's all over. He's not even wearing his wedding ring anymore. You have the last place in his life now. Oh, look he keeps avoiding you. He doesn't even want you to touch him…"

Chapter one

■

*Remember also your Creator in the days of your youth,
before the evil days come and the years draw near of which
you will say, "I have no pleasure in them"*
Ecclesiastes 12:1

I was 24 years old when I met Carl in 1993 and had
not been living according to my faith for over five years. I
hardly gave any attention to God at all. This, in spite of the
fact that between the ages of twelve and eighteen I grew up
in a strong Christian community. My brother and I began
attending a youth group of the Pentecostal Church, after
being invited by our neighbor. I soon noticed that the girls
and boys that went to the youth meetings were different
to those I had been accustomed dealing with. They were
joyful and exuberant and they didn' t swear nor did they
speak insulting or belittling words to each other. There
was something going on there that I had never experienced
before. There was something about these people that I could
not explain or describe. From the first moment that I was
with them I felt accepted and safe. The love that they had
for one another was indescribable and clearly had its effect
on me. I was able to be myself in their presence. It was also
the first time that I felt free in the midst of my peers.

There was happy singing and dancing during the youth meeting and for the first time I heard a sermon preached about Jesus, Son of God, that really impacted me. Therefore, already during this first youth meeting, I dedicated my life to God and got saved. From that moment on there was a dramatic change in my young life. I became more patient and I had a quiet peace inside of me, a peace that I've never known in my young life up till then.

When I was eighteen years old I left the familiar surroundings of life on my birth island Curaçao and moved to Florida, USA, for a four year Bachelor Study in Human Development. It was not long after that God stopped playing a major role in my life. Partying and dating began dominating my life. I even became pregnant during one of the relationships I had. I was 21 years old at the time and was just about to begin my Senior year in college. I was desperate and confused about what I was to do about this situation. But I clearly remember how I lay in my bed one night and promised my baby, that I would never get rid of him or her, tears rolling down my cheeks. Still, the pressure from my surroundings and the thought of the shame for my family of bringing a child into this world, unwed, made me break my promise to my baby not even two days later. I was four weeks pregnant when I had an abortion in a Florida clinic. From that moment on I had to deal with the consequences of my decision. It was not until years later that my true feelings about what I had done manifested in my life. It was also years later that I was able to ask God to forgive me for what I had done and it took another while before I was able to really forgive myself. In the meantime it helped that with the passing years the memory of my deed gradually faded...

After returning to Curaçao, at 22 years of age, I continued the lifestyle that I had started in the United States. It was not until meeting Carl two years later in the city of Zoetermeer, Holland that I settled down a little. I was living with my brother and sister in law at the time because of a recent breakup with a former boyfriend. My brother was a good friend of Carl's and it wasn't long before we started dating. Carl was not at all religious and as a result of that there was hardly any room for God, especially at the beginning of our relationship. We went to parties together regularly. Still, shortly before we decided to get married I started visiting church meetings again off and on. Carl even went to some of the meetings with me. We dated for two years and were married on July 07, 1995. Although Carl did not see the need for a blessing of the Church on our marriage, I insisted, and our marriage was blessed in a Pentecostal church in Zoetermeer, which we sometimes attended.

Besides good times, Carl and I also went through times of frustration and dissatisfaction on my side, from the very beginning of our relationship, I especially had a hard time dealing with all the time that Carl spent with his friends.

It made me feel insecure up to the point of me asking myself if I mattered at all in the relationship. I was also disturbed by the ease with which Carl went about with other women. I was always of the opinion that he was too 'close' with them. Because of this I was often jealous, insecure and frustrated, but Carl never thought it was any big deal. As a result of this I was often angry and disappointed in our relationship. Dealing with the situation was all the more difficult for me because already from a young age I had difficulty expressing and talking about things that bothered me.

So, in my eyes Carl was definitely not perfect. Still, in spite of this, our relationship to me was the most perfect one that I had experienced in my life up to that moment. In spite of my negative feelings and thoughts concerning Carl's behavior I loved him very much and we were inseparable. We idolized each other and Carl really believed in the strength of his love for me. Even when I failed and treated him badly he honestly kept on believing that his love for me would conquer everything that ever went wrong between us. Surely, this relationship was meant to last.

Chapter two

■

As a deer pants for flowing streams, so pants my soul for you, O God. My soul thirsts for God, for the living God. When shall I come and appear before God?
Psalm 42:1-2

About nine months prior to Carl leaving me I was determined to dedicate my life to the Lord again and live the way He wanted me to. I was out of a job for some time now and was therefore even more eager to do something worthwhile with my life, something in which God would play a central role. I wanted to do more than just visit church once in a while so I started intensely praying and reading books about God, His son Jesus Christ and the Holy Spirit.

The Bible says that when Jesus left this earth he promised those who believed in Him that He would not leave them as orphans (John 14:18). He promised to send us "another Counselor', the Holy Spirit. This same Holy Spirit would live with us and be in us for all eternity (John 14: 16, 17) and would remind us of everything Jesus said (John 14:26). He would not speak on His own but would speak all that He hears from God. He would also tell us about things that are yet to come and show us the way to the full truth (John 16:13-15). Because of all I learned I got a new desire for

God and I really wanted to make myself useful to Him and tell people about Him. Also concerning this, the Bible teaches us that it is the Holy Spirit who equips us to do so.

On a quiet morning in February, 1999 I cried out to God in our apartment in Curaçao. Carl had just left for work. I told the Lord that I wanted to meet Him, the Living God. I could hardly believe what happened after that.

Friday February 26, 1999

    Today I met the Holy Spirit for the first time. Even now as I mention His name He makes his presence known to me by way of a light tingling all over my body. It is as if He wants to remind me: "Yes, I am still here with you".

    For some months now I've been telling the Lord that I want to experience His presence, His anointing in my life. A few weeks ago I borrowed a book from mom called "The Helper" which was my first step in getting to know the Holy Spirit, Who He is and what He stands for. My dedication to the Lord grew because of what I read in this book. I asked the Holy Spirit to lead me and speak to me. I asked Him to make me sensitive to his voice and soon began noticing how He communicated with me in big and small things as a sweet voice in my spirit. Last night I was reading another book called "Good Morning, Holy Spirit". The author tells about how the Holy Spirit is gentle and full of love and that He never forces Himself on us. After reading this book I noticed that I was constantly talking to the Holy Spirit, even in my sleep.

What happened to me this morning is something that I will not easily forget. It was between 8:00 and 9:00 AM. After I woke up I prayed and told the Holy Spirit:"Lord, I want to meet You, but I'm so scared." I was afraid to have this unusual experience because I didn't know how He would reveal Himself to me. My growing hunger for His touch and revelation made me ask Him to come to me gently and quietly. I prayed in my bedroom and 'waited'. While I sat there talking to the Holy Spirit, His presence slowly began filling the room and I experienced a quiet peace. The atmosphere was so 'clean', so pure. I continued talking to Him and said: "Come Holy Spirit, come closer." With every word I spoke I felt His presence becoming more tangible. I started crying because it was so obvious that He was there with me, and just as I asked him He came oh so gently and peacefully. In tears I said to Him: "Holy Spirit, You're here, You're really here!" Even though there was not a doubt in my mind that it was so, I continued talking to Him and asked Him: "Holy Spirit, if You're really here, please touch my right hand." I stretched out my hand to Him and at that same time I felt a powerful warm tingle go through it. It was powerful yet not painful. After that I lifted up my left hand and said: "Holy Spirit, touch my left hand too." This continued until my whole body was tingling with His presence all over.

While enjoying His presence I softly began singing 'Holy Spirit, You Are Welcome In This Place', but now the song had new meaning for me. I no longer told Him that He would be welcome if He came, but with a thankful heart I was able to tell Him that He was indeed welcome, being there with me right there at that moment. The peace I experienced inside me grew deeper and deeper.

It's impossible for me to describe with earthly words how this felt, but the experience was warm and deep and real. I also had an indescribable joy and peace within me. It was supernatural. I've waited a long time for this day, but I never dared to think that it would actually happen. I thank You Lord for this newly found friendship with you!

Chapter three

■

Which was not made known to the sons of men in other generations as it has now been revealed to his holy apostles and prophets by the Spirit.
Ephesians 3:5

But the Helper, the Holy Spirit whom the Father will send in my name, he will teach you all things and bring to your remembrance all that I have said to you.
John 14:26

After meeting the person of the Holy Spirit He began showing me different aspects of Himself, of God the Father and of Jesus. He also made me more and more acquainted with the loving heart of the Lord Jesus.

The following notes give an impression of the insights I received during those days. They also reveal God's faithful presence in my life and how He placed a deep desire in my heart to tell others about Him. These revelations were given to me during Christian meetings, while reading the Bible or in my hours of prayer.

First day of Christian meeting in Trinidad

Tens of thousands of people came together under the open heaven to praise and worship the Lord. The speaker of that weekend opened the service with the song 'Holy Spirit, You Are Welcome In This Place'. It was not long before I experienced that unmistakable presence of the Holy Spirit again. I've been preparing myself for these two days for some time now in prayer. I longed to meet the Lord again. During the service I realized like never before that life is really all about Jesus. I realized that I would never lack anything once I had Him in my life. I don't have to beg Him to allow me to experience His presence, because this is what He desires for me and He longs to be close to us.

Second day of Christian meeting in Trinidad

What can I say about what I experienced today? What can I say about the greatness of my Lord? What can I say, except: "The Lord is worthy to receive all glory and praise. He deserves to be magnified!" While worshiping the Lord today I was very emotional and tears streamed down my face. I began sobbing deeply and was so thankful. It's all about the great love that God has for us. I realized this today like never before.

What great love He has for us who are just a speck of dust in comparison to Him. Out of pure love for us, God the Father decided to send Jesus to earth so that we would not have to experience hell. He did this out of pure love for us, who have done nothing for Him and often do not even recognize Him for who He is. Jesus was crucified for us, for you and me. He, being God's son, the son of the living God of the Universe, could have decided to put an end to His suffering, but He didn't. Out of love for us He went through pain and humiliation. While going through this He was thinking about us, He was thinking about me. Out of love Jesus sent the Holy Spirit so that we would never be left alone. And the Holy Spirit is concerned about every detail of our life and wants to lead us and help us in His own gentle and loving way. Today all I could think was: "Jesus, my dear Lord Jesus, how can we sometimes be ashamed of You? How can we not long to be used by You, to make others know You?" You give so much love. Thank you, my sweet Lord Jesus.

Desire to be used by the Lord

Lord Jesus, I love You and I have such a great desire to be useful to You. But Lord, in order to do this I need You. Your Holy Spirit needs to show me what it is that You expect and desire of me. Do not leave me alone, Lord. It is such an honor to be known by You. Teach me to always remain humble. Today I said to You: "Lord, it cannot be that my first encounter with your Holy Spirit was just a pleasant experience and nothing more than that." And right after saying this I heard one of your servants mention that the anointing gives us the strength and power to be able to fulfill

the work for Your Kingdom. Lord, You know my desires.
You also know my fears and my doubts. Please, make what
seems impossible, possible in and through my life. Use me
to bring people closer to You. Use me Lord and show me
clearly what I need to do. In Jesus' name.

Answers to prayer

I'm thankful to the Lord and I pray that I can continue growing
in Him daily. The Lord has been speaking to me directly
through His word for the past three days. It all started when
a few days ago I felt as if I was not accomplishing anything
with my prayers, asking God to use me. I told Him that I
didn't know what He expected of me and where I was to
start. After praying, I opened my Bible with a heavy heart.
While I was leafing through the pages, I felt the Holy Spirit
saying: "Stop! Read that verse". The words of Psalms 32:8
seemed to jump off the page in bright colors. This is what
I read: "I will instruct you and teach you in the way you
should go; I will counsel you and watch over you." This
experience made me realize that I could trust God to lead
me in the way that I am to go.

Two nights ago I called upon the Lord again. During
my prayer I told him that I felt as if I was wasting my time.
"There's nothing going on in my life", I said. A few days
ago a sweet lady I know gave me a book as a present, called
'God Calling'. For each day of the year there is a short
message. Suddenly I got the urge to read the passage for

the next day, right there and then. After reading the first few sentences I had to put the book aside, shocked and surprised as I was by what I read: "...Rest in My Love, walk in My ways. Each week is a week of progress, steady progress upward. You may not see it, but I do. I judge not by outward appearances, I judge the heart, and I see in your heart one single desire, to do My will. So, though you may feel that your work has been spoiled and tarnished, I see it only as love's offering. Courage, my child. Persevere, persevere. Love and laugh. Rejoice.

The realization that the Lord was so close and that He heard and answered my prayer awed me and at that moment I became small, silent and humble before Him.

The presence of God in my life

Last Wednesday I got a beautiful and clear revelation about the presence of God in my life. While I prayed and worshiped the Lord I thought about how God was carried around in the Arc of the Covenant by his people in the Old Testament. They carried Him around with them wherever they went. Then I realized that the New Testament says that I am a temple of the Holy Spirit (1 Corinthians 3:16). I no longer have to go somewhere to seek God. He lives inside me. And now I am His Arc and carry His presence with me wherever I go. This realization was so great and real to me that I prayed that the 'house of the Lord', my body, would always be pure, clean and without sin for the Lord.

The Lord loves us all

I notice that I've slowly been losing my humility since I began seeking the Lord more these past few months. My attitude, also my attitude toward the Lord became: "Look at how I'm seeking God to be used by Him. I'm so special." But these last days it really hit me that I'm not the only child of God whom He loves. I'm not more or better in God's eyes than anyone else. There are many others who sincerely love God and want to serve Him. The Lord even loves those who are not seeking Him the way He would like them to and He desires to be close to them. Who am I to think that I alone am privileged and that all the others matter less? The Lord loves His creation and is in love with man whom He created in His own image and likeness (Genesis 1:26).

A lesson about the love of Jesus

This morning I read Luke 6:37-38 where Jesus teaches that we must love our enemies, bless those who hate us and pray for those who treat us scornfully. A few hours later I went to get some groceries. While driving back there was a woman in a big, expensive car behind me. She had a terribly arrogant attitude about her and stuck to my bumper, because she obviously thought that I wasn't driving fast enough. I was annoyed and mad and began grumbling to her from my car, while looking at her through my rearview mirror. At a certain time she passed me in a most aggressive way and gave me a dirty look. I was angry and called out something ugly at her. But as soon as the words came out of my mouth the Holy Spirit exhorted me. Deep inside my spirit I heard the words: "Melanie, Jesus went to the cross for her also." I began talking to the Lord about this and in my anger I said: "Lord, how could You have done that. There's nothing loving about her. I would never have died for her." And the Lord showed me:"I did, because I love her." In my heart it became quiet. I thought back about the verses I read this morning and I thought of my own shortcomings and my ugly attitudes and I said: Lord, it must have cost You a lot to die for us, people, who sometimes show such ugly character. But because you did this, You expect the same from me.

I noted that the Lord sometimes expects us to do things that are almost impossible. Even loving our enemies is a practically impossible task, unless we do it with His help. Loving God's way will never be something we can do in our own strength. We need the heart of Jesus to be able to do this. A little while later I thought about how much the Lord did for me and how much love I received from Him. I thought about how He filled my life and how happy I was with Him. I realized that I wanted everyone, even my enemies, to experience what I have been experiencing with the Lord these days. I also want those people who openly provoke and mock God to understand what it's like to live close to Him and have a relationship with Him, and I prayed: "Lord, that woman in her expensive car, let her know You. Give her the opportunity to get to know You. Save her, Lord please!" And at that moment I realized that I was doing just what God desired of me. I was praying for this woman and asking God to be a blessing to her. This was only possible through God's power. Lord, You are so good!

Paul's simplicity of spirit

I'm reading Philipians 2 and I am encouraged by the honesty and simplicity of spirit with which Paul writes. I was struck by his pure and sincere love for the people in the different churches. In this, Paul reminds me a lot of the Lord Jesus. And I'm thinking: "We lack this today. Our love for each other is often so carnal. We try to be loving, we try to be good to our neighbor. We try to, but the Holy Spirit is showing me: "Stop trying so hard and just be rooted in me. Be rooted in reading My Word and meditating on it. Love me. Don't be so busy trying to be a 'good Christian' but be active in those things concerning Me. If you plant yourself at My feet, then My lifestyle and standard of living will automatically become visible in your life".

Jesus understands

I'm fasting these days and because of this my spirit is free to receive from God. These past days I have asked the Lord: "Lord, let me know You more, so that I can love You more." While listening to worship music the following dawned on me: Jesus came to earth to show understanding for us, people. He left all His glory and riches in heaven

38

to come where we are and understand us. He lived among us and therefore understands our pain, our hardships. He understands what it feels like to be abandoned and alone. He understands how difficult it can be to make the right choices, the right decisions. Jesus came to earth to go through what we go through, to feel what we feel. Jesus understands our struggles, He knows our weaknesses. He also experienced all these things, yet without sinning, so that He could be there to pick us up when we fall. Jesus understood that He had to overcome, for if He hadn't we would not be able to stand. And because he understands, He cries with us, He carries us, He helps us and gives us His love, His strength and His grace so that in Him we too can be overcomers.

I now understand the depth of Jesus' words: "I will never leave you. I will never forsake you." I now understand why He will never leave us. He cannot, for without Him we can do nothing (John 15:5). We need Jesus to help us through and He does. Jesus, I thank you for understanding.

No time for Jesus

Some time ago I was thinking about us, humans. We so easily say: "I don't have time to pray and read the Bible. Life is just too hectic and busy." But Jesus, He's the One who can say that He was really busy. He constantly had people around him, He was always busy healing someone, casting out demons, preaching and teaching God's Word.

He traveled from place to place on foot. He was busy, yet time and time again He made the effort to communicate with His heavenly Father. He did this either early in the morning or after teaching his disciples and others. He kept seeking God the Father's face and He did this for us.

Just imagine if Jesus would not have been in prayer daily. He probably would not have been strong enough to live a holy and blameless life. And where would that leave us? If the One who was to be the spotless lamb of sacrifice would have decided that He was too busy to seek strength through prayer from the Father? Jesus had to constantly pray to His heavenly Father. He needed the strength of the father to be able to stand His ground and overcome, every day again. He was not only perfect because He was the son of God, for, after all, He was also the son of man. He was powerful and without sin because He kept seeking the Father and gained strength out of that communion. If Jesus needed the Father that much, how much more do we!

Chapter four

■

*For I know that nothing good dwells in me, that is, in my
flesh. For I have the desire to do what is right, but not the
ability to carry it out. For I do not do the good I want, but
the evil I do not want is what I keep on doing. Now if I do
what I do not want, it is no longer I who do it, but sin that
dwells within me.*
Romans 7:18-20

*Let all bitterness and wrath and anger and clamor and
slander be put away from you, along with all malice.*
Ephesians 4:31

      Because of the time I spent with the Lord and my
relationship with the Holy Spirit I was spiritually on a
mountaintop. There was no doubt in my mind that God was
real and that He wanted to be involved in my everyday life.
I had experienced that He heard me and answered me when
I prayed and asked him for the things I needed and wanted.
Spiritually I was rich, but my circumstances looked really
bad. My marriage seemed to be totally falling apart.
After Carl's sudden departure my world came crashing
down. I was completely taken off guard and ended up sick
with pain and sorrow, full of questions and doubts, because:

"How was it possible that the man who once called me his 'princess' and also treated me as such, no longer wanted to be with me? How was it possible that the one who once would sacrifice anything for me suddenly felt nothing for me anymore? What happened? What had I done to Carl? How could our marriage of four years suddenly be over? How could it be that I never picked up signals that our relationship was coming to an end? I remember Carl saying to me, after he left: "You were my beginning and my end and everything in between." How could such a relationship ever end?

Shortly after Carl left me I did some soul-searching and discovered character traits and attitudes of mine that were not good, for example, getting upset when Carl went out with his friends. Another thing was that I sometimes reacted annoyed when he asked me to do something for him and that I often put myself, my needs and wants before his. I told myself that these were points in my character that I could easily adjust if only I would be more alert in the future.

As time went by it became apparent that it was not so much my growing faith in God that made Carl unable and unwilling to stay with me anymore. The real reason lay in my negative attitude throughout our relationship. Carl confirmed this to me. In spite of his great love for me, he felt more and more helpless when he realized that there were things about me that even his love for me could not change. But also concerning these things, I thought: "It will cost me

some effort, but I will be able to change. I can change!"
I was motivated to alter my attitudes and make an effort to adopt new attitudes and behavior that would benefit my marriage. I was going to do this together with God and was determined to make the most of the time that Carl and I were separated. I was optimistic and filled with hope as I looked forward to the day when Carl and I would be back together again. I asked the Lord to transform me and to teach me more about His love each day, so that I could learn how to apply it in my marriage in a practical way. Those friends of mine who were aware of my situation offered me books that would help and support me through this process. Of all these books there were two that particularly interested me because of their practical application, namely: "You Can Be The Wife Of a Happy Husband" and "The Five Love Languages"

My positive disposition made me 'know' intuitively that what I was going through was not simply a difficult period in my life, but it was a once in a lifetime chance to take a good look at myself, to learn and to change, with God by my side.

Tuesday October 12, 1999
It is only now becoming clear to me that there are things about me that totally turn Carl off, things that I keep doing wrong time and time again without realizing it. Carl made

it very clear to me some time ago that he didn't want to continue the relationship with me anymore. This hurts so much. Still, I am convinced that the Lord has a plan with all this and wants to shape and mold me into becoming a more mature Christian. If things had continued the way they were going, I would never have noticed my mistakes and had a chance to work on them. I've now received a wake-up call and am forced to come to terms with my shortcomings.

In the meantime I had gained some insight in certain things about myself that were not good. Yet, one day I decided to ask the Lord clearly and explicitly to reveal all those things to me that I was doing wrong in my marriage. It was as if the Lord was just waiting for me to ask Him this question so that He could finally give me the answers. As in a movie, the Lord showed me two important things. To make the first point clear to me He used the communication classes that I taught to parents and teachers, as an example.

Sunday, January 23, 2000
In my classes I teach parents that they need to have empathy for their children, that they must listen to them when they speak and want to express themselves. I teach parents not to counterattack their children when they're trying to tell them something. For, if the parent does this the child may become emotionally secluded when he is constantly being rejected, corrected or criticized. But not one moment in all those

years did I realize that I was not communicating with Carl the way I was teaching others to do. Oftentimes I did not even really hear him when he spoke. I listened, yes, but it was more listening out for something I could counteract. All those years I thought I was the perfect wife for Carl, always there for my husband. I thought we had a relationship in which everything could be discussed. When Carl flared up at me before he left, and said: "You never listen to me", I couldn't understand what he was talking about. "What do you mean I never listen? I always listen", I thought. But no, the Lord showed me that Carl often could not really express himself to me because of the way I reacted. As the years passed he withdrew from me more and more and eventually ended up sharing only non-threatening and pleasant things with me. It is now occurring to me that I displayed this same behavior a week or so ago without even realizing it.

I learned from this that I communicated poorly with Carl and didn't even really listen to what he said.

Secondly, I saw that I blamed Carl a lot and had many grudges against him:

Sunday, January 23, 2000
Every time Carl and I have a discussion I rip open old sores, blame him and keep bringing things up that were a problem in the past, things that Carl did wrong (in my opinion). I keep

45

blaming him for every mistake he ever made and stay stuck in the past. Deep in my heart I despise him for spending so much time with his friends when we first got married and for leaving me at home alone. I get angry at him when he says that other women are pretty. I know that I am critical and bitter when I do these things, but it is because I am especially unsure about the depth of his love for me and about what I really mean to him. I feel 'put aside' because he doesn't talk to me about the things that really occupy his mind. Sometimes I get the feeling that he doesn't want to give me his trust and doesn't dare to open up to me. I 'hold him in contempt' for his seeming indifference and for not being the way I would like him to be. As far as I'm concerned Carl is not allowed to make mistakes.

I am slowly realizing that I'm really doing the job of the devil by behaving in this way. The devil is the accuser (Revelations 12:10) and wants to keep reminding us of our former sin. The devil is the one who tells us that we don't deserve a second chance. Who wants to live with an accuser? Who wants to live with satan? But the Lord is different. He forgives us and helps us to go forward and this is what I need to be doing for Carl also.

I thought that the Lord was ready with me after this and that I had learned all that was to be learned, but I was wrong.

On Sunday, February 06, 2000 I celebrated my birthday. I

missed Carl very much, but my family meant a lot to me on that day. They spoiled me with presents and I got a lot of extra attention. Many of my friends called to congratulate me. In the days prior to my birthday I saw Mark, one of the witnesses at our wedding and Carl's best friend. Carl had spoken to him about all the things that were going on in our relationship and he flew over from Holland to talk to us. The talk I had with Mark was very clarifying.

Saturday, February 12, 2000
Mark told me that the relationship was definitely over as far as Carl was concerned. Besides my faith, now all my shortcomings from the past are playing a role. Carl doesn't see any possibility of solving all these problems anymore. In his opinion he has nothing to return to anymore. He is hurt to the core and accuses himself of having given me so much love while receiving so little in return and he's mad at me for having done this to him.

I went to my pastor to talk about the situation and we planned a day of prayer and fasting. Last Sunday I also spoke to a sister from church who is an intercessor. I asked her to keep praying for me together with the prayer team. I know that God has forgiven me for my shortcomings and now I want to continue pressing on so that He will also touch Carl and heal him from all the pain that I caused him. It hurts my heart to think of how Carl has sown into this relationship for years, but how he has given up on me right at the moment when the Creator Himself is dealing with me, and giving me a chance to thrive beautifully. Carl has gotten tired and has turned his back on me. My life has been shaped into what it is for a very long time. Now the Lord is dealing with me and 'pruning' me all at once. This pruning is causing me a lot of pain because almost all my 'branches' need to be cut off and new ones need to grow in their place.

After meeting Mark I had two dreams in which the Lord clearly spoke to me. The dreams confirmed to me that I often wanted to have my own way at any cost. They also showed me that I wanted everything in my time and at my terms and that I was often too preoccupied with myself. In the months after Carl left he mentioned those things to me several times, but it didn't 'hit home' as it did when the Lord revealed them to me through these dreams.

Friday, February 18, 2000
I just had two dreams. In the first one I was busy doing my housework while a little child hung around my neck, crying and screaming. I knew he was behaving this way because he was hungry. Still, I chose to finish doing my housework before feeding him. I wanted to prepare something special for him and wanted to be able to take my time to do it. It had to be good because then the child would be happy, I thought. But before I finally got the time to prepare his food, the child

was promptly taken away from me by another person, who gave him what he needed. This dream made me recognize that I do always want to give my best and I have the best intentions, but it has to be done my way and in my time. Because of this I often miss the opportunity to do good and as a consequence neither Carl nor I benefit from it.

In the other dream I was wearing a wedding dress with a train of at least 8 meters long. I was getting married, but there was no groom in sight. I was standing amidst many guests who all had their attention fixed on me. In the dream I was very much present and I had just sung a song for my guests. I was so impressed with myself that I announced to the guests that I was going to sing for them again. I was stealing the show. With all this, in the dream, I was not even aware that the groom was nowhere to be found. Was he hidden under my train?? Although I don't recognize this behavior as such in my daily life, I understand that with this dream God wants to show me that in my marriage, it's all about me.

Chapter five

•

*If I speak in the tongues of men and of angels, but have
not love, I am a noisy gong or a clanging cymbal. And if
I have prophetic powers, and understand all mysteries
and all knowledge, and if I have all faith, so as to remove
mountains, but have not love, I am nothing. If I give away
all I have, and if I deliver up my body to be burned, but have
not love, I gain nothing.*
1 Corinthians 13:1-3

A few days after having these dreams I bought an 'Amplified
Bible'. That same night I woke up at 3:30 AM and read
1 Corinthians 13:4-8 where the Bible speaks about true
love: *(4) Love endures long and is patient and kind; love
never is envious nor boils over with jealousy, is not boastful
or vainglorious, does not display itself haughtily. (5) It is
not conceited (arrogant and inflated with pride); it is not
rude (unmannerly) and does not act unbecomingly. Love
(God's love in us) does not insist on its own rights or its own
way, for it is not self-seeking; it is not touchy or fretful or
resentful; it takes no account of the evil done to it [it pays
no attention to a suffered wrong]. (6) It does not rejoice
at injustice and unrighteousness, but rejoices when right
and truth prevail. (7) Love bears up under anything and*

50

everything that comes, is ever ready to believe the best of every person, its hopes are fadeless under all circumstances, and it endures everything [without weakening]. (8) Love never fails [never fades out or becomes obsolete or comes to an end].

Monday, February 21, 2000
Especially verses five and seven of these Bible texts 'hit home'. I see that I am not at all the person described in these verses. As I read, I began seeing myself, as in a movie. I saw and experienced myself the way Carl must have seen and experienced me during periods in the years we were together. How horrible!
I saw how I sometimes put his food on the table for him with an unfriendly look on my face. I saw how with half-clenched lips I then asked him what he would like to have to drink with his meal. I saw myself sitting next to him in the car, squeezed all the way against the car door, as far as possible away from him because he had said or done something that I didn't agree with or that bothered me. I saw my anger, but I also saw how I was unable to express what I really felt inside. I saw myself sitting staring resolutely out the window, my arms crossed tightly over each other. I saw the day before me when Carl went out to get groceries by himself because I was so angry at him that I refused to go with him. I saw my own face before me when I was angry, and how often did Carl have to look at that face! I saw my

51

reaction when Carl had to come and pick me up and he was late. I didn't even care about how much effort he may have made to try to be there on time. The Lord showed me how these recurring behaviors made Carl ultimately tread on eggs. He was unable to live freely but became more and more careful, weighing and carefully considering every word he spoke so that he would not say or do anything again to set me off.

From all this I was able to conclude that my marriage lacked true Godly love.

One week later I came yet another step further in my learning process and was able to see the background and roots of my shortcomings, which became especially evident during my marriage. I clearly saw that I had not yet 'settled accounts' with events from my past and that these were of influence on my marriage. In my thoughts I was taken back to the time of my early childhood.

Before I gave my life to the Lord at the age of twelve, I was a very insecure little girl, because of how I looked. I was a little chubby, wore glasses and was so shy that I literally walked around the schoolyard with my head buried between my shoulders. I was often excluded by my classmates of the elementary school and had very few friends to play with. There were times that I would pass by groups of children from my class, hoping that I would be asked to play with them. On rare occasions I mustered up enough courage to ask if I could participate in their game. Yet, once admitted, I was too shy to get into the game like the other kids so I was still excluded from the group. I clearly remember that the school recess seemed like an eternity to me. I was always happy when I was sitting safely behind my desk again, but even there I fought my own quiet battle, always tense hoping that the teacher would not call on me to answer a question. I was grateful when the school day was finally over and I was able to go home. So, I was an insecure child with low self-esteem who also received signals from her surroundings that she was not worth very much.

From my early teens onwards, as I began attending the Christian youth meetings, things began to change. I felt more at ease with my peers. I felt safe in the group of which I was a part and my relationships with other boys and girls became closer. Suddenly boys also started noticing me and I got a lot of positive attention. Because of this I became more confident. I mattered. Others noticed me. While I sat thinking about these things the Lord led me to read through my old diaries. I noticed some things, and concerning this I wrote:

Tuesday February 29, 2000
As I got older, say from my eighteenth birthday on, I wasn't living the way the Lord wanted me to anymore. I seldom

attended church meetings and the Lord became less and less important to me. I began basing my self-esteem and the feeling of being worthwhile on the love and attention that I got from boys, and there was always a 'nice boy' on the scene willing to give me this attention. Whenever I did't get attention from boys or when I wasn't dating, I felt bad, lonely and worthless, because there was no one to affirm me. In those periods I reverted back to the old thinking about myself that I must not be very worthwhile at all.

The problem with my inferiority complex then was in fact never completely resolved, but was being covered from time to time under a blanket of 'positive attention from the opposite sex'. I had yet to deal with negative emotions from my past.

Tuesday, February 29, 2000
An added problem is that, while I was growing up, I never learned to express my feelings about those things that really bothered me. I kept my negative emotions to myself and bottled up everything inside. When it all became too much for me to deal with, I would lock myself up in my room and cry. There were also times that I threw fits of anger, walked away in a rage, destroyed objects or hurled them across the room. I never spoke about my deepest feelings and thoughts when in fact they raged intensely inside of me, unsolved and unspoken. Sometimes it would take days before I could

function somewhat normally again. I live my life and at the surface everything seems fine, but almost daily I struggle with my low sel-esteem and rejection from the past, before as well as during my marriage.

Hoofdstuk 6

∎

For my sighing comes instead of my bread, and my groanings are poured out like water.
Job 3:24

How unbearable it would have been for me if I had not gotten a diary as a present from my parents for my eighteenth birthday. My life-buoy became that, at least on paper, I was able to perfectly express my deepest emotions and write things off of me. Talking remained a very rare thing for me to do and this continued even into my marriage with Carl. Notes from my diary written in the fourth and fifth month after my wedding day are proof that I had in no way dealt with my negative past. My feelings of helplessness, not being able to talk about my emotions and thoughts and my inferiority-based doubts about what I was really worth to Carl, led to depression and desperation. My insecurities also caused me to become isolated, as I didn't take any initiative to have contact with other people. I was so alienated from God at the time that it never even occurred to me to include Him in my difficult situation and ask for His help. I just wandered around alone in my desperate situation and didn't see any way out.

(Flashback) Friday, November 24, 1995

I'm home alone again. I need to talk to someone but there's no one for me to talk to, so I'll just write again. I'm so tired of everything. I miss having my friends around. I need friends that I can go out with and have a good time with. Carl is out with his friends again, as usual, while I sit at home alone, talking to myself and hanging in front of the television. There isn't even anyone I can call to just have a chat with. I'm so lonely here. I think I'm too dependent on Carl, while he absolutely doesn't need me the way I need him. He's just as well without me, it seems, because he has all the things that I don't have, like his activities, his friends whom he sees often or who call him. All I have is Carl, and honestly, sometimes that just isn't enough. When things aren't going well between us, I'm completely on my own. I want to live again!!

(Flashback) Sunday, November 26, 1995

Today I lay in bed until 5:00 PM with heavy migraine. I feel so downcast and depressed all day. I'm insecure about everything, about myself and about the people around me. Talking is so tiresome. It seems as though it just makes the real problem drift away further. I don't know where I begin or where I end. This is how I feel, but I can't really explain it. I'm so sorry that I'm burdening Carl with my heaviness. Nothing is any good. I don't know what to do, because I don't know exactly what is wrong with me. Insecurity, low sel-esteem, that's evident, but how am I supposed to deal with it? I don't know. I want to be happy but everything is so uncertain. Sometimes life hurts. I don't know where all this is going. I don't know why it has to be like this. I'm going to bed now. I'll deal with tomorrow when it comes.

(Flashback) Monday, January 15, 1996
It seems as if I'm depressed every single day. I feel so locked up in myself. I can't even talk but my mind just keeps going off the whole day. I feel as if I'm drowning in my problems. There's no way out. Where's the beginning and where's the end? Everything is spinning around and around in my head. I feel so choked up in myself. There's no way out. I'm so tired, so sick and tired of everything, but especially of myself. What's wrong with me? The more I try to express what I'm thinking and feeling the more difficult it becomes to understand the core of my emotions and to clarify them. There are so many things going on inside of me at the same time. Sometimes I feel like I'm such a failure and I know I have nothing interesting to offer others, except problems and heaviness. I'm tired of the life I'm living. When was the last time I was happy? I mean really happy? When was the last time I felt like I could conquer the world and that I knew for sure that I was worthwhile and that I counted for something? I don't know where the answers are. How will I ever get out of this if I'm unable to express even my own feelings and thoughts? They're not even clear to me!

(Flashback) Thursday, January 18, 1996

I'm having a better day today than the last time I wrote. Still, the fear remains for the next time that things will go wrong. Carl was with his friends again today. He didn't even call to say that he would be home late. He got home after 10:00 PM. Do I matter? Does Carl still think I'm worth his while? I feel as though I am not here... I wish I was more needed in this relationship. It is very difficult for me to accept that Carl made a choice to be with me, but that he doesn't really need me in any way. With or without me he's just as content. It's stupid really, the things that one thinks at the beginning of a new relationship. I really thought that everything between Carl and me would go perfectly. It's hard to have to accept that a relationship hardly ever remains as good as it was at first. All beautiful things seem to come to an end. The less pleasant things will always be there and may even become worse. I know, it's all very depressing again but this is the way it is. I don't think I will ever be completely happy. Besides, I don't know if anyone ever really is. Life could have been a bit milder, if you ask me. Sometimes, actually quite often, I feel as if it would be less painful to go through life alone. There's not the pain of disappointment when there's no one to expect anything from. It's not easy being me.

My inability to change the situation weighed heavily on me. I disappointed myself time and again because of my failures, because I was depressed again, because I was unable to talk about what I felt and thought and because I was driving Carl crazy. I had crying fits and outbursts of anger that neither Carl nor I knew what to do with. I felt a mixture of pain and anger. Sometimes I laid doubled up in bed days and nights, rocking myself for comfort as tears streamed down my face. How often I thought: "I'm going to get up and go to Carl and tell him that I'm so sorry. I'll tell him that I don't want there to be any disagreement between us. I'll tell him that I'm sorry for hurting him. I'll let him know that I'm trying my best to be good but I'm just not succeeding in holding onto this good feeling." But even these words of apology were impossible for me to express.

And after such a negative experience, it was always Carl who came to me again to comfort me and to tell me that everything was going to be okay, because he loved me so much. And when the pain was gone and the mistakes forgiven, life would continue as if nothing had happened. Carl said it was okay, so it's okay, at least so I thought, until the next time that things went wrong again. This vicious cycle repeated itself continually and increasingly caused a lot of emotional damage in my life and in our marriage.

When I first got married I thought that Carl would fulfill me in everything and that he would make me happy. I clung to him for my security and my dignity. For me Carl had to be without fault and perfect because I had to be able to pull myself up on him for my self-esteem.

I'm finally realizing that this is the reason why I feel so horrible and angry in my marriage when Carl pays attention to others (be it a man, woman or his friends) or when he says too many nice things about someone else. He is supposed to affirm me, isn't he? But by being nice to others, he's giving himself, so that affirmation and positive attention that I need so desperately, to someone else. I now also understand that this is the reason why I become so irritable when Carl points out my mistakes to me, even when he does this in an atmosphere of love: My self worth, my feeling good about myself is completely dependent on his approval of me. So, I interpret every attempt that he makes to talk to me about what I could do differently or every spoken word that hurts me or that I don't agree with as:"He doesn't think I'm good enough. He doesn't think I'm worthwhile." I keep drawing everything back to myself in a negative way.

The Lord is now teaching me that no human being, not even Carl, will ever be able to fulfill me completely. He's also teaching me that I should never expect anyone to do this. For, by doing so I am placing that other person before an impossible task which he or she will always fail to fulfill. After all, true perfection is only found in God.

My entire life I had drawn on others for my self-esteem and this was something I had to stop doing.

Chapter seven

■

For the LORD your God is testing you, to know whether you love the LORD your God with all your heart and with all your soul. You shall walk after the LORD your God and fear him and keep his commandments and obey his voice, and you shall serve him and hold fast to him.
Deuteronomy 13:3-4

I was now aware that events from my past had influenced me but I proceeded to see something new that was closely related to drawing my self-worth from another: I had to learn not to place Carl, or anyone else in my life, before God.

In the days that followed I was constantly being confronted with the text in Psalms 139: 23-24: "Search me, O God, and know my heart; test me and know my anxious thoughts. See if there is any offensive way in me, and lead me in the way everlasting." I asked the Lord: "Show me Lord, what is not right in my heart."

In fact, I already know the answer but I don't want to admit it: God is asking me to let go of my 'idol' Carl who I have pulled myself up on for years. He's asking me to let go and surrender Carl to Him. He's not talking about a physical 'letting go' as in a divorce, but this is about a spiritual 'letting go'. In the meantime I learned that my joy in life is not dependent on Carl. Yet, he still occupies the most important place in my heart while the Lord wants to be the absolute only One to fulfill that place in my life.

As if to further convince me that I needed to let go of Carl, I received a phone call from a sister from our church. She said to me: "Melanie, read Genesis 22:9. This Bible verse is about Abraham who was willing to sacrifice his son Isaac, whom he loved so much, to the Lord. But Lord, how can I renounce Carl??

I started praying softly in my bedroom. After a long time of worshiping, I got up on my feet and told the Lord:

"Lord, I give Carl to you. Take him, Lord, and let Your will be done in his life, let Your will be done in my life and let Your will be done in this marriage. You're so good to me. You're so great. Let Carl know you, too. Let him experience Your greatness in his life. I thank you in advance for the miracle of salvation for my husband.

As I continued praying my prayer for Carl changed from: "Lord, bring Carl back to me", to: "Lord save Carl, save his soul!" After this prayer I ended up in a tiresome battle. On the one hand I surrendered Carl to God and said that I trusted in His plan, whatever this would be. But on the other hand I found myself taking the situation in my own hands and trying to win Carl back using my own strength and means. At times it was very difficult for me to keep my eyes focused on the Lord.

After these 'sessions' with the Lord in which He showed me so many aspects of my personality, I began asking myself if there was anything at all that I had done right in my marriage. I felt horrible for having caused so much misery in Carl's life and for not always being there for him the way I should have been. I also felt terrible that at times I got so angry at him. It was hard for me to admit to myself that apparently I had still not understood much about true love, after four years of marriage. "How could I not have been aware of all this?" I thought. On my knees and with tears in my eyes I asked the Lord to forgive me for all the mistakes I had made in my marriage.

I beg you Lord, to change me and to give me a new chance to do good in my marriage with Carl. For the first time I see the burden I have been to him during all those years. I only now understand what a difficult time he must have had all those years and I also now understand how much I need for him to forgive me. Lord, I pray that You will use me to warn others not to make the same mistakes that I've made.

The Lord had forgiven me, of that I was sure, but it would

take years before I could forgive myself for all I had done wrong.

The abovementioned series of events were my first steps in a process of personal restoration and healing by the Lord. In all of this it was with awe that I noticed the following: the Lord made my mistakes known to me, He confronted me with all the things I had done wrong, but not once did He point an accusing finger at me. In spite of the 'severe' way that He showed me my shortcomings and faults, He always remained gentle and loving in His dealings with me.

After this 'spiritual cleansing' I made an appointment with Carl. It was with enthusiasm but also in tears that I shared with him all that the Lord had shown me and dealt with me about.

Carl listened to me and when I asked him to forgive me, he took my hand and said: "It's okay, Melanie, you didn't know." That was all that came out of his mouth. Carl didn't say to me: "I forgive you", yet those are the words that I need to hear now more than anything else. I was disappointed and broken because I didn't get the reaction from him that I hoped for and expected. I now realize that I heard the words "it's okay" many times in the past. Now, looking back, it is obvious that it was not "okay" all those years and that there was indeed a lot wrong with my attitude in our marriage.

Chapter eight

∎

For the word of God is living and active, sharper than any two-edged sword, piercing to the division of soul and of spirit, of joints and of marrow, and discerning the thoughts and intentions of the heart.
Hebrews 4:12

In spite of Carl's dull reaction I still continued believing that it would not be long before Carl and I would be together again. For, I already knew what all the things were that I needed to work on in my character. But there was no change for the better after my appointment with him. On the contrary, it wasn't long after our meeting that he informed me that he definitely would not be coming back to me. As a result of this I was forced to leave our apartment and move in with my parents. The stress and loneliness of being alone in our apartment were too much for me to bear. As soon as I left, Carl moved back to our apartment.

The apartment feels cold and empty without Carl. We've spoken to each other a few times. Sometimes the talks we have give some hope but at other times they just rip me up inside with pain. Life has suddenly become very difficult for me. I want so much for us to be together again and for all to be well. I'm willing to correct my mistakes and even to change, am I not? But Carl doesn't want to come back to me. My heart is broken, broken for my husband whom I love so much. Lord, bring Carl back to me quickly, but if it's going to take a while before he comes back, then give me the strength to go through this. Help me, Lord!!

As I cried and prayed I thought about the story of Job in the Bible and how the Lord put His hedge of protection around Job and his family. I asked the Lord to protect me also. Later on I thought about how, like in the story of Job, satan was possibly saying to the Lord about me: "Take away her husband from her and see if she will not curse You to Your face" and the Lord saying: "okay satan, go ahead." (Job 1: 9-12). Satan needs God's permission to keep Carl and me away from each other. Because God has given His permission, I know that God is still the One in control.

I asked the Lord to reward me the way He had rewarded Job after his time of suffering (Job 42:10), a time in which Job did not deny his Lord. I promised the Lord that, in the same way, I would not deny Him, either. While I spoke out these words in prayer I experienced God's strength and presence again real close to me. I felt that I was being strengthened by Him again, from deep within, so that once more I could continue. Everything is going to be okay. I am going to make it. In Jesus' name.

A few weeks later I wrote:

The Lord is good to me but I need to constantly keep making a choice for Him and His word. Carl was supposed to call me yesterday but I didn't hear from him. I was broken and felt lonely. I got up from my bed and stood by the window. The tears streamed down my cheeks and fell like heavy drops on the night-stand under my window. I called out to the Lord and through my pain began speaking out God's promises. I said out loud that the Lord was with me and that He would never forsake me (Joshua 1:5). I said that I had put my hope in Him (Psalms 42:12) and that I knew that God would answer me and bless me (Jeremiah 33:3). I stood on God's Word and by doing this in faith I was lifted up out of my pit of heaviness once again.

Sometimes I receive strength for a day from the Bible, but there are also days when after a few hours or even minutes later I need to fill myself up again with God's Word in order to be able to stand. I'm learning to trust in God's goodness moment by moment and because of this I'm forced to stay real close to Him. I'm now very much aware of the fact that faith and wanting to serve and trust the Lord, is not solely a matter of how I feel. Rather, it is a choice that I must be willing to make daily, in spite of my feelings of brokenness and desperation.

I thank the Lord that I have Him in my life and that He knows my pain. I realize that He also knew loneliness, but many times worse, when on the night of His arrest every one of His beloved disciples had abandoned Him (Mark 14:50-52). I think about Peter and how he said that he would never forsake Jesus, yet he did. Carl also once told me that he would never leave me because he loved me so much, but still he did. I thank the Lord for standing with me in this difficult time.

With my newly found 'weapon' of confessing verses from the Bible, I began seeing small and great victories in my life. One night, once again I felt depressed because I missed Carl so much. It was as if I was about to drown in this feeling. But as soon as I began speaking out God's word, I was pulled right out of my low spirits. I confessed that God is able to do exceedingly more for me than I could ever ask or imagine (Ephesians 3:20) and that I knew that God had a future full of hope for me (Jeremiah 29:11). I told the devil that I would not remain cast down but that I would continue trusting the Lord. After this I started singing and praising the Lord. I was grateful that He had equipped me with His Word and with praise and worship to be able to withstand everything that came my way.

A few days after the above mentioned I went by Carl's apartment and I thought: "I wish Carl would come and get me. I wish the Lord would make it so that Carl and I would be together again soon", but then again, I thought: "No, the Lord is not ready with me yet and who knows what He still wants to do in Carl's life. I had every bit of confidence that the Lord would reunite us in His time and therefore I kept optimistically looking out for a good end(ing).

Still, as time passed I noticed that something had changed in the way I related to Carl. This is evident from the following:

Thursday, March 02, 2000
Carl has been away now for almost six months. A lot has changed in the past few weeks. I really want to be with Carl again, but I am now also complete without him, in the sense: I am not dependent on his presence in my life anymore to really be happy.

Not even a week later Carl confronted me with the news that he officially wanted to divorce me. I sought refuge by my brothers and sisters from the church. I also asked the members of the intercession team, which I was part of, to support me in prayer daily.

In the next Sunday service a sister from church prophesied over me that the Lord had seen my tears and the suffering of my heart and that He was there to help and to deliver. I was also encouraged by another sister, one of the intercessors in the church. Some months before, she also stood at the brink of divorce. Her husband didn't want to be with her anymore. Yet, at the last moment at the court of justice the Lord touched his heart. With tears in his eyes he told the judge that he didn't want to divorce his wife at all. Their relationship was miraculously restored. After the service this same sister told me that she was praying and asking the Lord to do the same for me.

Chapter nine

∎

No temptation has overtaken you that is not common to man.
God is faithful, and he will not let you be tempted beyond
your ability, but with the temptation he will also provide the
way of escape, that you may be able to endure it.
1 Corinthians 10:13

My soul melts away for sorrow; strengthen me according
to your word!
Psalms 119:28

One morning I was wide awake after having a disturbing
dream that just wouldn't let me go. I dreamt that I went by
Carl's apartment. He was not at home. There was a key ring
on the computer table and on it were a number of women's
rings. I went through the rings to see if my wedding ring was
in the bunch, but it wasn't. When, in the dream, I looked at
my ring finger, I saw that I was wearing my ring. What was
the meaning of this dream?

In the days that followed I noticed some unusual behavior
in Carl.

I drove by the apartment to bring Carl a Bible. I have the impression that he's not been home for some time. Where is he? When I saw him again yesterday he asked me in a very friendly tone to sign a document which says that we are financially completely independent from one another. He also wanted me to sign saying that he is the sole owner of the house that we are building. I'm sure that he's not being honest with me about the house, so I feel manipulated and trampled on. I have noticed that Carl can be sweet and accomodating when he wants something of me.

Some time after, Carl told me that in future he wants me to give him a call before passing by to visit him. He doesn't want 'any and every one' to be in his apartment when he's not at home. I felt small and humiliated when he said this to me. In a matter of a few months I have become 'any and every one' for Carl and I mean nothing at all anymore to the one who once loved me so much and with whom I desire to be so desperately. We've become strangers to eachother. Every time we meet I notice that we've grown further apart. Each time our dealing with each other is more harsh and distant. This is the first time since I know Carl that I don't trust him.

Friday, April 07, 2000
I've lost my joy and feel gloomy. There is an internal battle going on inside me which is even letting me be torn between my own desires and God's Word. I feel that I'm fighting

to hold on to my marriage just because the Lord says: "I hate divorce" (Malachi 2:16) and:"What God has joined together, let man not separate" (Matthew 19:6). As far as I am concerned I have no reason to desire this marriage anymore. I don't have any love for Carl anymore. How can I still love or want to be with someone whom I cannot trust?

Some weeks later there was another evening when Carl spoke to me calmly, but my distrust towards him which was very strong by then, made me be on guard: "What did he want from me? What's going to be the next incident?" I thought.

During that conversation Carl told me that he had had too much 'hassle' with me in the past and that he didn't want this anymore. He also told me that he has no feelings for me anymore. The flame he once had in his heart for me is now completely quenched and he doesn't think it can be rekindled again. To him, a relationship should flow effortlessly, but his feelings for me are completely blocked. He apologized for hurting me so much and said that he could see that it was making me suffer. This made things even harder for him. Carl wants me to find another man who can give me what I'm worth. But I don't want another man in my life. I'm still trying to convince him that things can work out between us. I begged him not to dwell on my mistakes of the past and to give the Lord a chance to save our marriage.

I told him about the testimony of the intercessor from our church and how the Lord had restored her marriage at the last moment.

I really did my best but it was all to no avail. And no more than three weeks later I was confronted with a gruesome and painful reality…

Saturday, May 06, 2000
This morning I went to Carl's apartment at 7:00 AM. I didn't call him first to let him know that I was coming. When I arrived there I saw a car parked next to his in the front yard. My heart beat wildly. I was almost dizzy with distress and feared what I might see when I walked into the apartment. Even before I reached the bedroom my eyes saw a horrible sight: through the wide open bedroom door, there was my husband Carl, in our bed, making love to another woman! Oh Lord, my husband is cheating on me!!! Oh Lord, my God…!!

It was then that I understood that the dream I had concerning the women's rings was a warning that I was no longer the only woman in Carl's life. Confused and with tears continually streaming down my face I ran back to my car. In a daze I drove to the house of a friend from church who lived nearby. I was in a state of shock when I knocked at her door on that early Saturday morning, crying and still trying to make sense of what I had just seen.

Even though Carl had made it clear to me more than once that he no longer wanted to be with me and that he no longer saw me as his wife, this experience felt like betrayal and hurt so very much. As far as I was concerned Carl and I were still a couple. This was just not allowed to happen!! I talked and talked and cried while my friend prayed for me. I stayed with her for a few hours until I had 'recovered' enough to go back home.

The most difficult thing in the days that followed was to keep my pain to myself. I didn't want to burden my dear parents with this almost unbearable news. They had already been through so much with me. I also didn't want them to start hating Carl.

Saturday, May 13, 2000
These days are so heavy for me. I cry days and nights. I don't even know what to do with myself. I'm hardly even able to write. My heart is in intense pain. I want to scream and cry out loud, but I don't want mom and dad to hear me and know my pain. For a few days now I can't eat and I have diarrhea. My hands and feet are cold and clammy all day long. I have such pain in my heart. I feel as if a part of me has been ripped out from my being, like something died inside of me and will never live again. I don't know how strong the Lord thinks that I still am.

Carl repulses me. I can't help but remember that one morning... I keep asking myself the question: "How could he have lied to me so easily?" I doubt everything he ever said now. I have no confidence anymore, not even in what used to be. What else has he not spoken the truth about? How can I know when he's telling the truth and when he's lying to me? I don't want to have anything to do with him anymore. I stopped wearing my wedding ring since last week. I cannot and do not want to be connected to Carl anymore.

This morning I was broken before the Lord. I lay on my face before Him but was not even able to utter one word to Him. I only hoped that the Lord would understand my pain and help me. I couldn't say anything and was not able to express what I was feeling inside. While laying there I remembered the Bible verse in Romans 8:26 and I cited it. I asked the Holy Spirit to intercede for me because I was not able to at that moment. When I picked up my Bible later on and began reading from it, I slowly felt the Lord's comfort and strength flowing back into my life. I worshiped Him in the heavenly language and thanked Him for strength to go on. Still, the pain of abandonment and rejection remain a real and harsh reality that I need to fight my way through, daily. I am only able to do this with the help of God's Word and through prayer.

Sunday, May 14, 2000

I thank you Lord for strength to go on. These days are tough and very unkind, but You are faithful. You are with me, of this I'm sure. Lord, I'm not asking You: "How long, Lord, how long do I still have to endure this way of suffering? But I'm asking You Lord, give me the strength to endure. Give me strength, give me patience and a strong shoulder to carry this burden for as long as it takes. Let it be so, Lord, that You receive the glory from this." I have never suffered like this before. I never thought I'd have to go through what I'm going through today. I remember asking You last year: "Lord, use me for Your Kingdom!" I didn't realize at the time that I would have to go through the fire first myself, and I never thought that this experience, being abandoned by my husband, would be my trial.

Chapter ten

.

How long must I take counsel in my soul and have sorrow
in my heart all the day?
How long shall my enemy be exalted over me?
Psalms 13:2

By day the LORD commands his steadfast love, and at night
his song is with me, a prayer to the God of my life.
Psalms 42:8

The incredible thing about this whole experience was that I
never knew before that God could be so close during difficult
times. All the things I went through left me no choice but to
cling to God and not to Carl. Slowly my desire to be with
Carl became secondary to my desire to live really close to
the Lord each day. When I went by Carl's some days later
to bring him a recording of a message I had heard, I didn't
know how to react to him. My emotions flashed from anger,
pain, disgust and complete repulsion, to compassion and
back again.

I went to Carl especially to bring him a tape with a message
on it with an appeal for him to allow God into his life. He
promised to listen to the message. He just called me to tell

me that he listened to the tape and prayed but that nothing had changed in his life. He said that he's so ashamed of what he had done that he doesn't even dare to look me in the eye anymore. He feels tired and empty inside and doesn't think there's any hope for him anymore. Even I have little hope left and I'm angry and frustrated.

Thursday, May 18, 2000
Lord, Carl doesn't want to be helped. What am I still waiting for then?! It's all too much for me now. I'm tired and honestly, I think divorce is the best solution now. Why do You let the enemy have his way for so long? Look at how many people are praying, Lord! When will You say: "Enough!"

The next Sunday I had a hard time in church. During the praise and worship I ran out of the church building crying. Once I got home I felt obligated to tell my parents about the divorce procedure that Carl was busy with. I told them that I 'suspected' that there was another woman involved in Carl's life. I didn't dare to tell them what I had seen with my own eyes only two weeks earlier at the apartment.

Even after that horrible experience of May 06, 2000, I was unable to emotionally and mentally loose myself completely from Carl. I was forced to keep praying and asking God to help me. One night I drove to the large parking lot of a shopping center in the area and cried out before the Lord. I cried tears from the depth of my being for my dear husband. I begged the Lord to help Carl and to heal his emotions that I had destroyed. I asked God to show him a way out. I begged God to be merciful to Carl and to forgive him for his sins. I pleaded with the Lord to please help Carl. I wanted so much to be able to do something for him but there was such a breach between us, that helping him became impossible.

There came a time once again that I began praying and asking God to show me what He was planning to do with my life. I was turned down for a job in Curaçao once again. This time it was a job at a Christian organization in which I really thought that I would be able to serve the Lord. I didn't get it. I cried and told the Lord that it seemed like He didn't love me. But then on Sunday, June 04, 2000 during the church service something really wonderful happened: I received an awesome Word from the Lord, which confirmed my desire to make Jesus known to others, a desire that I had discussed with the Lord many times before.

Sunday, June 04, 2000
When the service was almost finished my pastor called me forward. He prophesied over my life in front of everybody and said: "This past week the Lord has spoken to me concerning you. You will be sent out to bring lost souls into the Kingdom of God. Some will be easily reached but others will be more difficult. But your joy will be found in this, for

this is that which the Lord has called you to do. By the end of this year you will have more clarity concerning the next step that you must take."

Many people came to me after the service. They hugged me and rejoiced with me over the word that I had received. Some of them cried for joy and thanked the Lord together with me. It was awesome! My best friend happened to be in the church service that day. I remember telling her that the Word I received seemed to insinuate that Carl and I would not be reunited again. "But Lord, do something mighty in Carl's life so that he can no longer deny that you are God. Let him get saved, be baptized in water, be baptized in the Holy Spirit and let him fall completely in love with you!"

It feels like my life has direction again. I am joyful and full of God. Lord, from the bottom of my heart I say to You: "Even if everything is taken away from me, Lord, as long as I have You in my life, I have everything!! I want more of You. I want to be closer and closer to You.

And from that Sunday, June 4th, I began experiencing a special anointing in my personal life whenever I prayed or shared the Word of God with others.

Saturday, June 17, 2000
Last night was a really blessed night. First, I went to a prayer meeting at the home of an acquaintance and afterward I joined my own church for a prayer vigil. While I prayed, the

presence of the Holy Spirit was on me very strongly and my hands seem to be charged with electricity, just like when I met the Holy Spirit for the first time. When a friend of mine, Lucia, came to pray for me she said that she could feel the anointing of the Holy Spirit so strong on me. She spoke out in prayer that I was a chosen child of God, set apart for a special task. She prayed that God would use my hands and that they would be hands of healing. She also prayed for Carl that he would one day become a preacher of God's Word.

Friday, June 30, 2000
Carl doesn't interest me at all right now. At this moment I'm in no hurry at all to have him back in my life. Maybe the Lord knows that the only way to get me to spend time with Him and with His will for my life is to take away my 'wife-feelings' for Carl. I do want to see Carl come to the Lord, though. Lord, let Your will be done.
These days I spend hours alone in my room, with the Lord and with my Bible. I get to know Him better every day. I had many questions for the Lord about my way of praying. As I am on the intercession team of our church I often find myself in 'prayer warfare' and wrestling with the enemy for the needs of others. But I notice that I was missing something during my personal time with the Lord. I was led by the Lord to pray and fast together with my sister in law and a friend. I heard how they approached the Lord

in total dependence when they prayed. It was intimate and beautiful. They kept saying things like: "Lord, I beg You. Lord, I'm asking You, please…" I then realized that this was what I was missing in my personal prayer time. In the years passed as an intercessor I had learned to rebuke the devil with authority, but in doing so I had forgotten that I could also go to the Lord in total dependence for my personal needs. God says in His word: Do not be anxious about anything, but in everything, by prayer and petition, with thanksgiving, present your requests to God. And the peace of God, which transcends all understanding, will guard your hearts and your minds in Christ Jesus. (Philippians 4:6-7). It was great to be reminded of this truth again.

Since I began praying in this way, my personal prayer life became deeper. I had many things to thank the Lord for, to talk to Him about and to bring before Him in total dependence upon Him.

Tuesday, August 01, 2000
It is worthwhile being alone these days. If Carl and I would have been together today, I would not have had the chance to get to know the Lord as I am now. I also wouldn't have had such intimate contacts with other Christians (brothers and sisters) with whom I could talk so openly about all kinds of things, but especially about the Lord. Tonight at the prayer meeting we had a beautiful time of prayer. I was also

able to share with the others all that the Lord was doing in my life. I was able to testify of His greatness and encourage those present. I am so thankful to Him for this.

Today I went by a friend's house to take back a book that I borrowed from her. We spoke about how God uses situations (she herself is divorced) to shape and mold us so that we could be complete and full of joy. We also talked about how God was preparing us to be good wives for our (potential 'future') husband. I can hardly get over how I've grown in the last few months. I notice now that I used to be empty and 'young' before. Today I can rejoice and enjoy "Melanie" and the person I am becoming in the Lord. I'm becoming a whole different person now, spiritually in the first place, but also mentally and emotionally I am now so much more whole, stronger and richer.

Wednesday, August 09, 2000
Last night I met an old friend of mine with her husband and their two children. They are on vacation in Curaçao. It was great seeing them again, but at the same time it was a bit hard for me to be around them. They are 'happily married' and kept talking about their kids and all that they did together. For a minute I thought: "Lord, at this moment I have no husband and no kids. This hurts. I want to have these blessings too." And for a little while there I felt very lonely.

Saturday, August 12, 2000

In spite of everything I have peace in my heart and I trust that the Lord has full control of everything concerning Carl and me. Still, sometimes I struggle with the thought whether I could ever love Carl again. Right now I only feel compassion for him. He's not at all someone I want to share my time and my life with as a partner anymore, while Jesus, He means really everything to me!

Yesterday I told my sister in law that it is almost scary the way God is fulfilling me. Besides that, I think it's awesome that I have all the time in the world to spend with the Lord. What a privilege to be able to spend hours alone in my room with the Lord and to get to know Him deeper and more intimately each day. How great it is to be able to wake up in the middle of the night praying and singing and reading from my Bible without having to explain to anyone what I am doing and why. I'm free in and with the Lord, free to seek Him and to serve Him. I don't need anyone to fill my life. Jesus fills me, surrounds me, supports me, carries me and protects me. He is my all in all!! What a privilege, ...but... the Lord also knows that I want this to only be a season in my life. I would like to be happily married again someday with a man who rejoices at the very name of Jesus, a man who is on fire for the Lord and knows how to love his wife. I would also like to have (a) kid(s), and all this shouldn't take too long anymore, considering my age: I am almost 32!

Chapter eleven

■

What is my strength, that I should wait? And what is my
end, that I should be patient?
Is my strength the strength of stones, or is my flesh bronze?
Have I any help in me, when resource is driven from me?
Job 6:11-13

For a while there I was caught off guard: Carl called me
suddenly and said that he wanted to come by. I was nervous
because I didn't know what he wanted or what he was
coming to do.

Moments later…

Monday, August 14, 2000
Carl just came by. How strange! He told me, with a big
smile on his face, that he wanted to apologize for being so
stiff with me during the past year. He also apologized for not
having been a very good person to converse with. He says
that he started Transcendental Meditation a month ago and
feels that it is helping him a lot. I told him that I was happy
that he was doing better. I am happy that we were able to
have a normal conversation. "Lord does this meeting mean
anything? I place all this in Your hand again and I thank

You for all that You're going to do for Carl and myself.

While I prayed for Carl after we met, I had a vision of him kneeling next to the pulpit in a church with the Bible in his hand and his arms outstretched toward heaven. "Lord", I said, "forget Transcendental Meditation. Carl will serve You and live for You."

I had a great day at the beach with some of my friends yesterday. We arrived there at 1:00 PM and didn't return home until late at night. It was a lot of fun in spite of me being the only single person in the midst of only couples. I hardly know what to pray and ask God for concerning my marriage anymore. I no longer have the urge to ask: "Lord, let us be together again". I cannot force myself to ask the Lord to preserve something of which I am becoming more and more convinced that it is no longer what I want. This makes praying for Carl and our marriage very strange for me and makes me feel somewhat 'disconnected'. Lord, help me. I just don't know what to do about this anymore.

Not even two weeks after Carl's 'surprise visit' there were horrible days again. He called me and tried to convince me to give him a copy of my passport so he could arrange the divorce. I was overcome once more by feelings of being manipulated and humiliated. I called Lucia and asked her to support me in prayer. She called me the next day to tell me that she would like to have a talk with Carl to try to encourage him to allow God to deal in his life and in his situation. She also wanted to ask him if he could discontinue the divorce procedure for a while. Lucia wanted to know if I had any objections about her calling Carl. I told her I didn't. The meeting between them took place but had no effect at all. Shortly after, I got a call from Carl again with the same request as before.

I am torn in two: On the one hand I don't want to cooperate with a divorce in any way, because I don't believe that God supports this. On the other hand I often get such a feeling of disgust whenever I think about Carl that I would like to be released from him sooner rather than later. I can't imagine this marriage ever becoming something again in which we can be happy. It is also hard for me to imagine ever being able to experience Carl as a blessing in my life again. I can't understand why he is so determined to continue his plans even after hearing God's word many times and after I have asked him for forgiveness so many times. When Lord, when will there finally be a breakthrough?! What ever this may be!

My desire to 'obey' God and not co-operate with the divorce made me call Carl to tell him this. I told him that I didn't want to do something that I couldn't back up because of my faith. In that same conversation he made it clear to me in a very harsh tone that again it was all about what I wanted, what I felt and what I thought. He was cold and clearly let me know that he didn't have any desire to be with me anymore and that he was unable to force himself to feel otherwise. I broke (down) and in an outburst of hatred and pain I decided to immediately provide him with the necessary papers for the divorce. I had been on this 'roller-coaster' long enough now and I just wanted to get off!! I was tired of the pain of constant humiliation. Besides, the emotional strain that I felt, the fight between wanting to quit on the one hand and wanting to persevere and hope for the best, on the other hand, often seemed more than I could bear.

Saturday, September 16, 2000
The hand of the Lord is weighing heavily upon me. I can't go on anymore. Today I noticed that Carl's decision to divorce me, in itself, is not the main reason for my brokenness. My greatest hurt comes from the way he treats me, his manipulative way and how he speaks to me so nastily and unfriendly. My own husband is treating me like dirt. I also realize that I feel bad and guilty because it is my doing that has made Carl become so ugly and mean. Besides that, I have a hard time dealing with the pain I feel every time I speak to him and notice that nothing in his attitude has changed. Today is exactly one year ago that Carl walked out on me. This can hardly be called a marriage anymore. I'm not going to church tomorrow. I'm not in the mood for

happy people around me. I want to know what to do with my life. I'm sick and tired of Carl and think he's a real 'loser'. I have no more strength left to fight. Enough is enough!

In the midst of all this I thought back to a conversation I had with a friend a few days earlier, in which she said to me: "Do you know what a privilege it is to have to go through so many trials? It means that God's eyes are fixed on you in an incredible way! He's working on you with His own hands and is molding you to become more 'Jesus-like' through these difficult times. "This may be so", I thought, "but it's no fun at all!" Shortly after that conversation, the Lord by His mercy, showed me four important things during my time of prayer:

1. The Lord does not expect that I will never feel defeated and dejected. If this were so His Word would not say that He is the One who lifts up my head (Psalms 3:3).
2. The Lord supports me with different portions of His Word whenever I go through the valley. He shows me that His word is Truth and that it gives me strength to make it through every situation.
3. I need to look only to the Lord. He is the One and besides Him there is no God (Isaiah 45:5). He keeps reminding me of this.
4. My greatest prayer for Carl must always be this: "Lord, reveal yourself to Carl and let him see your greatness. Open his eyes."

Wednesday, September 20, 2000

Today Wednesday, September 20th, I had a rough day, but I've been strengthened by a long visit with Lucia. I just got home and am now enjoying a book I bought last week "the Bible Handbook". One of the Bible studies in this book talks about how God's people suffer (sometimes unjustly), but that they reach maturity through trials and distress. This is found in 1 Peter 2:19-20, 1 Peter 4:13-16 and 1 Peter 5:10. Now that I'm reading these Bible verses I find myself thinking back to my conversation some time ago with my friend: What a privilege, the eyes of the Lord are on me ...

Lord indeed, if the Christian life were only a bed of roses, how could I be a blessing to the world? If I only walked on pink clouds with You without ever knowing anything about pain and suffering, how could I mean anything to anyone? But now I've also known pain and I can direct others to the One who makes everything bearable: Jesus! For how supernatural is the way that You totally restore me and raise me up by way of your practical Word, every time I go through tough times. If I had not known difficulty in my life, I would never have known that this was possible. But now, in spite of my difficulties I'm still able to experience the supernatural and be joyful, satisfied and intensely happy in my heart. The only determining factor that makes this possible is my confidence in the Lord Jesus and His word. Lord, I thank You for this!

Hoofdstuk 12

A man's steps are from the LORD; how then can man understand his way?
Proverbs 20:24

In the meantime it was six weeks since I had seen or spoken to Carl.

Saturday, October 14, 2000
As time passes by I'm being loosed from Carl more and more and I'm forced to make the best of being by myself. An acquaintance of mine in Holland encouraged me to make a sudden decision: I am leaving for a long vacation to Holland next month. I'm not really enthusiastic about it, though. Holland has never attracted me at all, but I do have the need to leave Curaçao for a while. I hope that my planned vacation will do me good. This morning I put away everything that has to do with Carl, far away where I can't see them any more: Pictures, my wedding ring, gifts that he bought me... Everything! It made me feel heavy for a while but that feeling was soon gone.

At the same time I spoke to God and said:

Saturday, October 14, 2000
Lord, my life is one of many goodbyes, many new beginnings,
but little continuity. In fact, right now my life seems very
lonely. I don't feel this way every day, but when I look back,
I think: "What has really been permanent in my life, except
mom and dad whom I keep falling back on every time? This
cannot be the reason for my being in this world. When will I
go forward? When will I stand where I need to stand? Lord,
lead me into my purpose!"

Not even two days later there was a total change in me.
Suddenly I was excited about my trip to Holland.

Monday, October 16, 2000
Since this morning I'm excited about my trip to Holland. I'm
scheduled to leave on November 9th and I can't wait. The
joy I have is so great that I feel like I'm going to explode on
the inside. This morning I remembered the word I received
from my pastor last June. It suddenly came to my mind that
he said that I would be able to tell what the next step of
God's plan for my life would be, before the end of the year.
And now it's almost the end of the year and I'm planning to
leave for Holland.
Yesterday I read Mark 10:29-30. These verses tell about
Jesus' disciples and how they left everything behind for

the sake of the gospel and followed Jesus. Could this be what's in store for me? I want to serve the Lord. I want to be made ready to proclaim the gospel, give love to others. Father, help me and lead me and please take care of my dear, precious family that I will be leaving behind here in Curaçao. Show me the way as You promised me two years ago when I read Psalms 32:8.

Monday, October 23, 2000
The past days have been spiritually dry. I have a hard time relaxing and taking time to read God's Word. It's probably because of my excitement about my upcoming trip. Nevertheless, I still experience moments of complete awe when I think about the greatness of my Lord.
I am obviously physically still very much burdened with the whole situation concerning Carl and our divorce. I went to my house doctor today because of a heavy pressure in my head. He told me it is tension headache. It seems like all the tensions of the past year want to manifest themselves in my body all at once. My doctor is pleased with my intention to leave Curaçao for a while. He gave me a prescription for some medication to help me relax and gave me something to take for my headache, but he warned me that I had to make sure and deal with the cause of my condition.
After leaving his office I met an acquaintance that I had not seen in a long time. She knew that Carl and I were not together anymore, but when she saw me she was amazed at

how well I looked. She kept repeating over and over how she thought my face was beaming with happiness. Indeed, I do look very good these days, even though I say so myself. I am beaming and I am happy. My heart is happy. Whatever still needs to be solved and mended inside of me will all be dealt with at the right time. The Lord has proven enough to me to let me know that I can trust Him for this.

Right before leaving for Holland I was privileged to be part of a special experience which convinced me once more that my heart's desire was to share the hope that Jesus gives, with those who are brokenhearted.

Friday, November 03, 2000
Last Tuesday I was at the woman's ward of the Curaçao prison with "Taking it to the Streets", a group of intercessors, dancers and singers from Jamaica. We had the opportunity to minister to the prisoners for two hours by way of song and dance, testimonies and preaching God's Word. After the message I was also invited to pray with the women and offer them some personal encouragement from God's Word. Many of them were crying because the Spirit of God was so clearly present at that place to touch them at the point of their need. While being there, I thought: "Lord, this is the kind of work that I want to do for Your Kingdom: to love people, to encourage them and edify them with the hope that You give."

After the meeting I spoke to two of the intercessors. One of them said to me: "I am not one to sit in church." At first I didn't understand what she meant and I was disappointed because I thought she was a Christian who 'worked for the Lord' on her own and didn't see the need to be part of a local church. But soon it became clear what she meant, as she explained to me that she receives her spiritual nourishment in church, but then sets out to minister to people in hospitals, prisons, shelters and relief centers. She said to me: "The Lord said: "Go" and I went. It's the people out there who need us, Melanie. So we must go" (Mark 16:15). Lord, You've shown me several times that I need to be involved in something where I can give a lot of love to others and really minister to them. The command to "go" has also been given to me, Lord, and I want to go. Please, prepare me for this.

Before leaving for Holland I also had two great days with my friends in Curaçao. They really did their best to spend as much time as they could with me.

Lord, bless them all. I'm dreading having to face the cold in Holland, but I hope it will not be as bad as I expect. I pray that I will get some clarity in Holland concerning the direction I need to take with my marriage, with my life. Lord, I know that You will not forsake me. I believe that this is a trip with a purpose, a mission in itself.

Thursday, November 09, 2000
I am in the airplane now. We will be landing in Holland in about one hour. Thanks to my niece and nephew being present at the airport in Curaçao, saying goodbye to mom and dad was not as difficult as I expected. That is, it was not overly emotional. I promised them that I would be back in Curaçao in March of next year. I told my family to see this trip as a long vacation for me. I thank God, for it is by His grace that I'm able to make this trip.

Chapter thirteen

∎

I will instruct you and teach you in the way you should go;
I will counsel you with my eye upon you.
Psalms 32:8

The LORD will command the blessing on you in your barns
and in all that you undertake. And he will bless you in the
land that the LORD your God is giving you.
Deuteronomy 28:8

After reaching Holland I stayed, among other places, at my
good friends Paul and Nayla in the city of Assen. They were
also good friends of Carl. It was pleasant and familiar to be
with them, yet I noticed that I missed Carl very much under
those circumstances: In the past Carl and I had always been
together whenever we visited Paul and Nayla.

I came to Holland to put everything behind me for a while,
but it seems as though it's all even more difficult for me,
being here. This morning I woke up with heart palpitations
and my spirit was heavy. I cried while Nayla sat with me.
She asked me if I didn't think it was a good idea to still keep
in touch with Carl, but 'without expectations'. She's afraid
that the distance between us will only grow bigger, now that

I'm in Holland. She also fears that this will stand in the way of a possible reconciliation. I don't know if I'm able to do what she's asking and if it will work. All I know is that I and everything that has to do with me are of no interest to Carl anymore. He just wants me to leave him alone.

A few weeks later I noticed that, slowly but surely, things began to change. My being in Holland made it easier for me to start focusing on myself and take my distance from Carl. After having been under so much tension for so long in Curaçao, being in Holland made me feel totally free. I was able to think clearly and objectively about important issues. God used Paul and Nayla to help me make difficult but necessary decisions. All this time I had it in the back of my mind that I would immediately return to Curaçao if there were any signs of Carl wanting to be with me again. Because of this thought I remained divided between two continents for a long time and was unable to make plans for my future, be it in Curaçao or in Holland. After one of my many conversations with Paul and Nayla, I finally made the decision to remain in Holland for a longer period of time. Even though I fully backed up this decision there were still doubts sometimes. More than once my heart cried about all the mistakes I had made in my marriage and I asked myself if there would ever be a second chance for me. But over time I was able to rest in the knowledge that the Lord would go His way both with my life and with Carl's.

Saturday, December 02, 2000

I need to definitely accept that my relationship with Carl is over. Emotionally I'm not 'ready' yet to return to the situation I left behind in Curaçao. This means that I will have to start building up my life here in Holland, starting today. The very thought of this is really scary to me, but there have been 'first times' before for me. If I'm really honest, I must say that I'm looking forward to making a fresh start with my life.

I miss mom and dad a lot, but my poor financial situation makes it impossible for me to buy a telephone card to call them. I don't even always have money to pay my bus fare. I'm going through tough financial times and I'm completely dependent of the goodness of others. Still, I try not to see my financial dependence on others too grimly and I decided that I will not complain. I thank the Lord in advance for better times.

In the first few weeks that I was in Holland I couldn't find a job in my field as social worker, so I accepted several different jobs through an employment agency, just to be able to make a start in providing for my own needs. During the past six weeks I worked in the sorting room at the post office, at a child day care center and in the canteen of a technical university.

Sunday, December 10, 2000

Of course there are still days that I have my doubts about having left Curaçao behind me for a longer period of time, but Paul tells me: "Melanie, think about what you want to do, make a decision, execute it and don't keep returning to the subject. He's teaching me not to make decisions that are based on my emotions as they will seem right at the time, but the next day they won't anymore. When I make a decision my basis needs to be: "What do I want and where is God leading me to?" And this, notwithstanding what others want me to do or think that I should do. I have never had to take a stand on such important issues. Paul and Nayla keep reminding me that, whatever happens, God will always be with me to help me, support me and comfort me.

One night after another emotionally exhausting day I went to bed thinking that the Lord is really stretching me to the fullest. Paul and Nayla were out for the evening and I was home alone. I called out to the Lord for help and put on a CD. I worshiped the Lord and sang along with the songs on the CD. One of the songs was called "I love to love You, Lord" and the lyrics say: Lord I'm not here to complain about my many problems. By your spirit and your grace, I'm confident You'll solve them. But, I'm here, to say "I love You." In spite of my emotions and doubts I began thanking the Lord for every blessing that I had received from Him up to that point. I thanked Him for how He had lifted me and helped me through the past year. I thanked Him that I was able to know for sure that He would continue to be there for me, and that I could trust Him for his continuing guidance. Before I knew it, His peace flooded my life once more. I thanked Him for this. I could rest in Him.

Some good friends of mine from the city of Eindhoven invited me to spend the Christmas holidays with them. So, I took the train from Assen to Eindhoven. As soon as I stepped out at the train station in Eindhoven I felt an unusual attraction for this city. Besides that, I soon felt very much at ease with the people I met there. It had never before occurred to me to live in Holland, let alone in Eindhoven. But it was not long before I made the following decision: Eindhoven was to be my new home in Holland! I arranged to rent a room from the sister of the friends who had invited me.

One month later…

I got a great job through the employment agency as 'Raadsonderzoeker Strafzaken' (an advisory function to the judge and district attorney concerning criminal offenses of youths between the ages of twelve and eighteen) with the Child Welfare Council in Eindhoven. Finally I have a job on my level of education that I can really get into. I'm enjoying my new work environment to the fullest and I'm getting a good salary. My colleagues are great, the job is exciting, and it is low stress at the department where I work. Lord, I thank You for this!

Another month later...

I'm getting a permanent appointment at the Child Welfare Council and I'm soon required to follow an intensive internal course. Sometimes I just feel like praising the Lord at the top of my voice as I go to work. Even though I have no clue about what the future holds for me, I still feel like I'm standing right in the middle of God's plan for my life. In the meantime I am registered at two different housing associations for a rental apartment.

I often ask myself what this year has in store for me and what will be the things that I need to conquer and learn. I need to braise myself because by now I know that the Lord is not shy in using His 'pruning shears' in my life. I will now extend my stay in Holland indefinitely. I called mom and dad to inform them that I will be going to Curaçao for a few weeks vacation in April 2001. They're happy that I'm doing so well in Holland but have a hard time coping with the fact that I will not be going back to live in Curaçao for the time being.

Chapter fourteen

■

As obedient children, do not be conformed to the passions
of your former ignorance, but as he who called you is holy,
you also be holy in all your conduct.
1 Peter 1:14-15

On January 07, 2001 I heard a sermon in the Pentecostal
church in the city of Tilburg which I attended with my
friends from Eindhoven.

Sunday, January 07, 2001
The pastor spoke about God's people who were led out
of Egypt: At first, when the people complained God kept
showing them His greatness, by performing signs and
wonders. But after some time He began destroying them
when they kept complaining and He finished them off. In
doing so He was saying: "You have all seen my signs and
wonders and you should be mature enough by now to trust
Me and believe in Me." So, after showing His power God
really does expect His people to have faith in Him. He
wants us to know who He is and to begin to walk with Him
based upon this trust. As we mature spiritually the Lord also
begins to treat us differently as He takes on a 'no nonsense'
attitude towards us. There will be things that He allowed in

our life before that He will no longer tolerate. He will also want us to put aside and move away from things that we used to do in the past.

I had never dared to think that I would experience the reality of that sermon in my own life not even one month later. It so happened that I had a brief affair with an Englishman who was renting a room at the same house where I was staying. His wife had left him for another man and he was trying to make a new beginning with his life in Holland. I paid an extremely high price for my mistake: my intimacy with God was lost. I became more and more frustrated in my daily life, while bitterness and depression slowly began creeping in.

I grieved the Holy Spirit deeply with my sinful behavior (Ephesians 4:30). My choice to give in to sin has separated me from God (Isaiah 59:2). The intimate relationship that I once shared with the Lord and had cherished so much during the past year is completely gone. I lost His closeness and don't feel free in His presence anymore. My joy is gone and I'm plagued by feelings of heaviness and frustration. The Lord seems so far away. I can hardly even pray anymore...

Four weeks later...

Monday, February 26, 2001
Today is the first time since I'm living in Eindhoven that
I feel lonely and cast down. I'm also thinking of how I'm
getting older and I still have no kids. I don't know if this will
be granted to me anymore. I feel desperate. Also, there are
no prospects of anyone with whom I really want to share my
life. My own husband doesn't want me any more. Right now
everything seems dark and gloomy.

Another six weeks later, and I was still frustrated and far
away from my God. Mistakes that I had made in the past
suddenly began surfacing in my mind and made me feel
harshly condemned. Among other things, I was confronted
with the emptiness, the pain and the senselessness of my
abortion of almost eleven years ago. It was as if I was being
forced to come clean about my actions and experience them
all over again. I mourned my unborn baby for the first time,
with a pain and wailing that came from the very depths of
my heart and begged the Lord to please forgive me for this
horrible thing that I had done.

Monday, April 02, 2001
Where is all this going to? What in heaven's sake is the
purpose of all this? I'm tired of everything. I wanted so
much to have a child but apparently this is not reserved for

me anymore. Besides, with my 32 years of age I honestly don't think that it's necessary anymore, anyway. If only I had kept my baby then... None of my friends who have become pregnant out of wedlock are suffering now. No one seems to be pointing an accusing finger at them for having a child and no husband. On the contrary, they all have their children today who are a joy and a blessing to them. But no, I just had to go the other way and now I'm standing here empty handed and with an empty heart. What's this life of mine worth anyway? Is it my purpose in life to be constantly confronted with the consequences of my past mistakes? I feel rejected and abandoned by God. I feel as if God has turned His back on me while He blesses and smiles upon everyone else. This is horrible! What's the purpose of all this? When will it end?!

I'm reading a book called 'the Ministry of Intercession' and it's getting me frustrated. There are a lot of good things in the book but it frustrates me that God always seems to be one step away from me. Over and over I read about just that one thing that I need to do to be able to pray effectively, and I'm just not able to do it. It says very beautifully that we need to do everything by and through God's grace, and not in our own strength, but it just doesn't seem to be working for me and remains an unattainable pursuit for me again and again. The easiest thing for me right now is to just stop talking to God altogether. I don't seem to be doing it the right way, anyway, and I'm not getting answers to my prayers again anymore. So, I stopped praying for some time now.

In the same book I read that Jesus says: "...therefore I tell you, whatever you ask for in prayer, believe that you have received it, and it will be yours. (Mark 11:24), but what seems to be the problem? Melanie does not seem to really desire anything. So, when I come to God with my weak little prayers, saying: "Lord, I don't really know ... just let Your will be done, because I don't really know what I want", then God is probably scratching His head thinking: "Well my little child, what do you suppose I do with this? If you don't even know what you want to ask Me for?!" And then I realize that there is nothing that I desire so strongly anymore to make me bring it daily before the throne of God. I have even let go of my marriage which was once my greatest prayer request. What's more, I don't even really have the need for a relationship right now.

Today I am also angry at God because of two things: Why am I always separated from my family and friends? Why am I always by myself at every family event, without a husband or boyfriend by my side? Why must I always be alone with no partner and no family and friends? Is there a reason for this and if there is, why doesn't the Lord make it clear to me what it is? If there were something in it for me, for example the fulfillment of my one great desire to be used by God to tell people about Jesus (Hey, this is what I desire.....) then maybe it would all be worthwhile.

And so while writing down all my frustrations, the Lord still reminded me of my great desire that He had placed in my heart years before: to tell people about Jesus! I was able to see it in a flash in spite of my struggles and pondering. Even though my life with the Lord was not as good as it should be at that time, still in His grace He reminded me that His plan for my life had remained unchanged, despite my imperfections. That to me was true grace! I continued battling in silence and called out to the Lord to help me obey and serve Him the way He wanted me to. I realized as never before how much I wanted God to remain at the very center of my life.

I beg You for forgiveness, Lord. I long so much for our communion to be permanently restored again. Please, be merciful to me and help me to do again what is right in Your eyes.

Still for a long time after that the gap between God and myself only seemed to get bigger.

Chapter fifteen

∎

Return, O faithless sons; I will heal your faithlessness.
Behold, we come to you, for you are the LORD our God.
Jeremiah 3:22

Ask, and it will be given to you; seek, and you will find;
knock, and it will be opened to you. For everyone who asks
receives, and the one who seeks finds, and to the one who
knocks it will be opened.
Matthew 7:7-8

Two weeks later...

As I promised my parents I returned to Curaçao for a vacation
in April 2001. After this first visit there were many more to this
beautiful island. For a long time I had mixed feelings about this
first trip, because nothing at all had changed in the situation with
Carl. I didn't hear a thing from him anymore and therefore had
no idea where I really stood in relation to him. On the Friday
before I left Holland I organized a day of prayer and fasting with
a small group of friends. We prayed for Carl's salvation and
for my stay in Curaçao and put everything in God's hands. My
prayer life still wasn't what it should be, so I didn't get as much
out of our prayer time together as my friends did.

My friends advised me not to let the situation with Carl ruin my vacation. The Lord will work things out the way He thinks is best. We have prayed, fasted and cried out to God for His help and guidance. That is the most important and only thing we could do. The rest is up to Him.

Now, in Curaçao, I'm still far away from God and I miss His joy in my heart. I saw Carl once during this vacation while we were both in the traffic. My heart pounded in my throat. "Watch him go..." I thought to myself, "watch him go...". It breaks my heart to see how our relationship is slowly withering and fading away. I try to be tough and say that I will go through life alone, if I have to. But deep in my heart I desire a different life. I feel defeated!

I returned to Holland in the second week of May 2001. Saying goodbye to my parents, family and friends in Curaçao was heartbreaking. On my way back to Holland I felt empty, worthless and low-spirited. The Lord was distant and I missed His guidance. It was terrible. Besides, what was I really going back to Holland for? I couldn't think of a good reason. I got there on an early Friday morning. The next three days I didn't eat anything but only lay in bed, feeling completely hopeless.

It took at least five months for me to regain my intimacy with the Lord after having asked Him for forgiveness of my sin and after having turned away from it. During this time I kept begging Him daily to come close to me again. Restoration of my relationship with the Lord came suddenly after months of frustration and feeling that He had left me to myself. One day while I was praying I suddenly felt that I was being lifted and supported by the Lord again, like before. Once again I felt free in His presence and was able to sit on my Heavenly Daddie's lap without any hindrance. Once again I was able to share my joys and sorrows with Him, and draw from the intimate relationship that I had grown so used to over the past year. It was only then that it really became clear to me that my sin was the cause of this tiresome and barren period in my life (Isaiah 59:2). The restored relationship between the Lord and myself came just at the moment that I had to prepare myself for the next bump in my life.

Wednesday, July 04, 2001
I was shocked when I received a registered letter today from the clerk of the court in Curaçao. The letter said, among other things, that I had malevolently walked out on Carl, while he was the one who walked out on me!! I cannot help but think that this sentence which is based on a lie has everything to do with the splitting up of the ownership rights of the house that we are building in Curaçao. I have very little knowledge of legal matters, but I imagine that I possibly have no rights to the house if it proves to be true that I was the one who wanted to end the marriage. I'm not

at all interested in the house but what I'm reading is making me very angry. I must react. I can't leave it at this!

The letter also said that the divorce would be pronounced on September 4th, 2001 and that I would have the chance to defend myself. Making use of notes from my diary I made an orderly report for the judge of the events right before and after Carl's departure.

I'm thankful to realize that I'm emotionally quite distant from the situation. Thanks to the grace of God I don't feel humiliated and hurt, like I used to before. I'm relaxed and I know that it is only thanks to the Lord. My boss at work is giving me all the support I need. I will be flying to Curaçao for the court hearing on August 31, 2001.

A great blessing in between...

Wednesday, July 18, 2001
Today with a grateful heart I told the Lord that I don't lack anything in my life right now, except having my own rental apartment. I just called mom in Curaçao and asked her to pray and fast together with me for this. My decision to specifically ask the Lord for an apartment was prompted by a Bible verse that I read this morning: "Until now you have not asked for anything in my name. Ask and you will receive, and your joy will be complete" (John 16:24). We

114

will pray and thank God in advance for His answer and we're asking Him to send His answer before the end of this month...

And God answered our prayers in a miraculous way. Exactly one week later, on Wednesday, July 25, 2001, I was informed by the housing association that I was assigned a beautiful home in a quiet neighborhood in Eindhoven. I would get the keys on August 16, 2001. I could hardly believe the news. "Lord", I cried out, "How great is your mercy!"

Still, in the meantime the upcoming divorce procedure that was planned for September 4th, continued to occupy my mind and I had at a lot of questions for the Lord.

Thursday July 19, 2001
Is my marriage going to end on September 4th? Is that going to be it for me: "life goes on and better luck next time?" Lord, is this where it all ends, a divorce?! Then I ask myself: What for? I'm not bitter or angry. I am not even disappointed, but shouldn't every experience I go through eventually lead to something positive? The most positive thing that would bring glory to You, Lord, would be a miraculous restoration of my relationship with Carl. A "they lived happily ever after" ending. But this isn't even what I want anymore. A year or so ago I wanted nothing less. So, therefore again my question:"Lord, what for and what now?

Lately I've often mentioned how happy I am with my life and with You and that I don't lack anything. I was even talking about this to a colleague today. What a difference compared to some years ago when I felt worthless and useless unless a man was part of my life. And now I think: "Was this the purpose of it all? Was it to teach me that You alone can really, truly fulfill and enrich my life or is there more to this experience?"

Back in Curaçao...

Saturday, September 08, 2001
On Tuesday, September 4th, 2001 the judge pronounced the divorce. It was dad who ended up representing me at the court hearing, as it was still too much of an emotional burden for me to be confronted with Carl in that situation. What can I say about all this? I'm glad that I've already gone through a greater part of 'mourning' and learning to cope with the situation. I've tried to save my marriage during the past two years. I cried many tears and prayed many prayers, yet they yielded no result. Carl never came back to me. I finally got to the point where I could accept that my marriage was coming to an end, while living in Holland. I was even quite able to emotionally distance myself from the situation. So, in fact very little had changed for me on September 4th, except then, that the judge had also declared that what was once a marriage is now definitely over.

I didn't come to Curaçao with the idea that the Lord may still save our marriage and turn everything around. Yet, I can't help but feel unsatisfied, as if the enemy has won, as if Satan is rejoicing because he got what he wanted. My marriage is over and Carl is continuing his life as if nothing has happened. Lord, I don't know You as a God who allows the enemy to triumph just like that. This can't be the end! It's not possible that this is why I got married: simply to get divorced again?! There must be more to this. Lord, I want to see Your victory!

In the third week of September, 2001 I was on my way back to Holland again. Knowing that I now had the privacy of my own apartment to process all that had happened in the passed weeks, was very comforting to me.

Chapter sixteen

∎

All these with one accord were devoting themselves to prayer, together with the women and Mary the mother of Jesus, and his brothers.
Acts 1:14

After my return to Holland there was a 'Day of Refreshing' at our church on Saturday, October 27, 2001. There, once again, I received a Word from the Lord.

Saturday, October 27, 2001
It is now the second time that a prophetic word has been spoken over my life. I can't remember everything that was said this time, but I do remember these words: "The call of God is upon your life. I, the Lord, have seen your tears. Do not look back at your past anymore and put your feelings of guilt behind you. I, the Lord will restore your dignity. I break the works of witchcraft and evil words that have been spoken over your life." There was much more said but these were the words that stuck with me.
I'm now thinking back about the anointing of the Holy Spirit. I remember that day in 1999 when, after meeting the Holy Spirit, I wrote: Lord, this first encounter with You cannot be just a pleasant experience. There must be more to it. Shortly

after that, I remember hearing a sermon in which the pastor said that the anointing, the touch from the Holy Spirit, is to equip us to fulfil our God given task on this earth. I desire nothing more than to know God and to serve Him and to tell people about Him and what he has done in my life up till now. Could this be my task and the call of God on my life?

I began praying about this and asked the Lord to make things clear to me. Within five days I received, not one, but three confirmations that I should use my diary notes as a basis for a book to tell people about the power and love of Jesus in my life. I asked the Lord to give me time, patience, and discipline and requested Him to show me the way and the right timing to begin with my book. In the meantime I continued with my daily activities in Holland. I experienced some awesome things and was being continually molded to be able to be useful to God. Still, the battle within me concerning Carl kept on raging and actually seemed to have gotten more pronounced after the divorce. Especially in the month of February 2002, I noticed that I had not yet let go of my past and my broken marriage. I suddenly had a great desire for a second chance with Carl. I wanted more than anything to prove to him how much the Lord had changed me. I wanted to prove that I was still able to be a good wife to him. On March 11th, 2002 and April 3rd, 2002 I prayed about this and on both these days I received a sudden phone call from Carl, within 30 minutes of my prayers.

I made use of the opportunity to ask Carl for forgiveness one more time. I told him that I ended up hurting him because I didn't know better. I also told him that the divorce was a very high price that I was paying for all the mistakes I had made in our marriage. During the second telephone call he let me know that I really did hurt him a lot and that he hated me for this for a long time. But now he says that it is totally over and that he doesn't have any negative feelings or thoughts towards me anymore.

I mentioned to him that I was soon planning to go to Curaçao on vacation again. After hearing this he asked me to please get in touch with him as soon as I was on the island because there were some things that he wanted to discuss with me. His voice sounded serious when he said this.

These two telephone conversations I had with Carl convinced me that the Lord had answered my prayer for a second chance with Carl with a "yes". But first, before my planned trip to Curaçao, there was a very special experience in God's presence.

Sunday, March 17, 2002
Today I went to a church meeting in the city of Rotterdam with some friends of mine. The word of God flowed richly and touched our hearts. The sermon was about knowing Jesus personally if we want Him to use us, and Lord, do I

want this! We learned that even the disciples who walked with Jesus for years needed to have a revelation of who He really was: "Jesus Christ, the Son of the Living God" (Matthew 16:16). Jesus' supernatural power and might can become visible in and through our life when we know who He is.

After the service a few of us were invited for lunch at the Pastor's house. There was an atmosphere of unity and love in the home and all we spoke about was God's greatness. At a certain time the pastor said that the fire of the Lord would descend when the church of Christ would pray. After these simple words we all stood to our feet and began praying fervently to the Lord. It was not long before His presence was noticeably in our midst as we prayed in turns for that which God laid upon our hearts. Once again I felt His touch in my hands but this time it went even further. Right before my turn came to pray it was as if I was completely on fire on the inside and a surge of electricity seemed to shoot through both my arms. I prayed fervently like I had never prayed before in my life. I prayed for Satan to take his hands off all those who were destined for the Kingdom of God. I prayed for dedication and holiness among God's children. I heard myself praying but was hardly able to recognize myself. It was a prayer from deep within that could only have been inspired by the Holy Spirit. The Lord was close to us and there is no doubt that He heard our prayers. We just returned to Eindhoven, full of the Lord. It's now late at night.

The following day:

Monday, March 18, 2002
This morning I woke up with a thankful heart. I thank the Lord for all He has done and for who He is in my life. While on my knees in the bathroom I just told God that I want to completely turn my life over to Him and that I wanted Him to use me for that which He has destined me. "Lord, I want to remind You that you must not let Carl return to me if our being together doesn't fit in the plan You have for my life. I want to walk in obedience to You and I ask You to help me do this."

Chapter seventeen

■

The Lord is not slow to fulfil his promise as some count slowness, but is patient toward you, not wishing that any should perish, but that all should reach repentance.
2 Peter 3:9

I have told the glad news of deliverance in the great congregation; behold, I have not restrained my lips, as you know, O LORD. I have not hidden your deliverance within my heart; I have spoken of your faithfulness and your salvation; I have not concealed your steadfast love and your faithfulness from the great congregation.
Psalms 40:9-10

On Thursday, April 04, 2002 I landed once again on my beautiful island Curaçao. It was as if I had never left.

Thursday, April 04, 2002
As we agreed I called Carl soon after reaching Curaçao. We made an appointment for coming Tuesday, April 09, 2002. I am nervous and uneasy because I have no idea what he wants to talk to me about. It's been almost a year and a half since I met Carl for the last time.

Five days later, the day…

Tuesday, April 09, 2002
With knocking knees I went to the little cafe in the center
of the city where I had agreed to meet Carl this afternoon.
He was already there when I arrived and greeted me with a
big smile. He looked relaxed and happy. After a few nerve
wrecking moments in which I had to get used to being around
him again, we started a calm conversation with each other.
I'm back home now but I can still hardly believe what just
happened. Carl surprised and delighted me first with the
wonderful news that he had given his life to the Lord two
months ago. "My prayer has been answered", I thought,
"Carl has decided to live for Jesus!" But not even seconds
later my joy turned into disgust and bewilderment when he
added to this news that he had fallen madly in love with
the 31 year old Christian girl who had led him to the Lord.
She was the one who encouraged him to have an encounter
with me. She told him that he must return to me if he noticed
that he still had feelings for me after meeting with me this
afternoon. This then, was the reason why he called me twice
while I was in Holland. I can't believe this! I'm furious and
disappointed and I feel that he has made a fool of me. I was
lured into this conversation as a test case and now I just
have to deal with the end result of their little experiment, in
Carl's own words: "Now you are nothing more to me than
a beautiful woman for whom I have absolutely no feelings

anymore". Lord, I thought you had restoration in mind for Carl and me. Now it seems I couldn't be more wrong!

While driving back home and once I reached home my head was spinning. I had just enough left in me to thank God for Carl's salvation, but something didn't seem quite right, and I spoke to the Lord about this too:

Lord, I thank you for this miracle of salvation for Carl, but why does this testimony seem to be ending so crooked? Aren't you the God who is able to do even greater things than I could ever ask or imagine (Ephesians 3:20)? Aren't you the God who makes all things new (Revelations 21:5)? I know that salvation is the greatest miracle that can take place in a person's life and I'm really happy about this. But every prayer for restoration of our relationship now seems to have been left unanswered and wasted. I know that what is happening now is part of Your perfect will but know, Lord, that right now I'm full of questions: "How can Carl surrender his life to You, (something I asked You for in prayer) and then still decide to continue his life with someone else? Why did You allow for Carl to call me twice right after I prayed to You to give us a second chance together? Why do you 'arrange' a meeting between us if it is not in Your plan to bring us together again?" Lord, give me the answers I need. In Jesus' name.

Strangely enough after meeting Carl that day my hope for restoration of our relationship became even greater. I called Lucia and we discussed the situation for a long time.

Lucia is also of the opinion that we need to keep on praying about the current situation. I'm asking the Lord to show me by His Holy Spirit how I should pray. Lord, give me direction and let me know what Your plans are for my future on a personal level, if indeed Carl is to share his life with someone else. I know that whatever You decide will be best, but I also need to know and see WHAT it is. I also need to know what You really think about all this: "Was this divorce what You wanted? Am I obeying You if I conform myself to this divorce or do You expect me to continue fighting for a new beginning with Carl? If we both have to go our separate ways then I want You to make this clear to me and I want it to be Your decision, not a decision made by me, Carl or his girlfriend."

This whole situation bothered me so much that Lucia and I made an appointment to talk to Carl's Pastor who also knew me. He knew that Carl was divorced, but all this time he wasn't aware that I was Carl's ex-wife. After talking to the Pastor he agreed to give Carl a call that same day. The Pastor also knew Carl's girlfriend very well and told me that he was very fond of her. Yet for the sake of the faith he said that he would prefer if the relationship between Carl and me would be restored. However, he did make it clear to me that he couldn't force Carl to do anything against his will.

That day I prayed that Carl would understand that my talk with his Pastor was not meant to put a rope around his neck, but that I really needed clarity on this matter.

Lord, in spite of all the questions I still have and in spite of not knowing what the meaning of all this is, I still notice that You're filling me with inner peace. Glorify Your name and protect Carl also from unnecessary pain. Work out in him what needs to be worked out and do the same in me. I thank You for Your faithfulness and for standing with me in this situation.

In the meantime I intensely enjoyed my parents and friends during my vacation in Curaçao. Though very brief I even had a somewhat normal conversation with Carl, right before meeting with his Pastor. I was very curious to know what became of 'our' house that we were building, so I made an appointment with Carl to pass by and see it one afternoon. The house was almost completely ready and looked nice. I was truly happy for Carl that he was able to get through with the house and saw how proud he was of it. I noticed, though, that seeing all this didn't have any emotional impact on me at all. I didn't even feel a bit jealous or bitter when he told me that he was going to be spending the weekend at his girlfriend's. Was the Lord going another way with us or was

He just protecting me from unnecessary pain?

Towards the end of the vacation I began getting a better understanding of why it was necessary for me to meet Carl at the café and afterwards at his home. These encounters made me realize that things were really completely over between us and that I also needed to carry on with my life. And if I was completely honest with myself: nothing in me desired to have Carl as my life-partner anymore. I had no difficulty at all with the fact that he had a girlfriend, even though hearing the news hurt me anyway: my pride was hurt. So, the desire to be with Carl was no longer there, but how contradictory it was that the urge for restoration of my marriage remained. I couldn't make sense of it all and since this last vacation on more than one occasion I was overcome by feelings of anger and resentment toward Carl. My contradictory feelings forced me to return to the feet of Jesus time and time again with my questions, but also to ask Him for forgiveness for my anger towards Carl.

I just couldn't understand what was going on inside my mind, but the Lord had already planned a day in September where He would make everything clear to me.

The vacation continued and I went to a prayer meeting with Lucia. While we were all chatting with each other at the end of the evening, Lucia as well as the other women who attended the meeting told me that I should use my talents to bring people closer to the Lord. I decided right there and then that I would sing for my Lord and give my testimony for the very first time in the next Sunday service, using notes from my diary as a basis.

Sunday, April 28, 2002
Today I sang two songs and gave my testimony during the English service at the church that mom attends. I told the congregation about my life since Carl left me. I wanted them to know how difficult a time it was for me, but more than that I wanted them to see the greatness of the Lord through it all. I told them that the Lord was always faithful to me and that He kept giving me joy and strength to go on, because I learned to trust in His Word. I told them about the comfort I experienced when I desired so badly to have my husband with me and read in the Bible that the Lord, the Most High God said to His people Israel and also to me that HE is my Husband (Isaiah 54:5). I explained to them that God wanted to be all that they needed, too. For example, He lets those in financial need know that He is their provider" (Phillipians 4:19), to those who are sick He says: "I am your healer" (Exodus 15:26). To those who feel broken and defeated, He says: "I am the one who comforts you" (Isaiah 51:12). I encouraged them to take God at His Word and to trust Him for everything they needed.
I shared with them how sometimes God chooses to leave our circumstances unchanged or to let them turn out

differently than we expect. In my case, Carl never came back to me, but the Lord had changed me. I went from a woman who thought she had to have the acceptance and love of a man to be worthwhile, to a woman who knows that she lacks nothing in her life once the Lord God Almighty is at her side. I had learned to be dependent on God and not on men. I now knew I had everything, really everything, in God and that He also had good things in store for Carl.

I explained that, to me, 'victory' no longer meant that the Lord would take me out of the storm and bring me safely to the other side. True victory has become to me that I could trust in God and His Word in the midst of the storm and experience His supernatural strength either to stand firm and wait or to move on. I ended by saying that I was glad that I had gone through all of this because it has given me the opportunity to encourage and build up others in the Lord. I said that I had only now realized all that God was capable of and that I was happy to be able to share this with others.

The response I got during and after giving my testimony was overwhelming. Apparently, the people were touched deeply in their hearts and many of them cried. Even some men were unable to contain their emotions and were in tears. After the service many came to thank me for the encouraging testimony and to tell me that they were strengthened by it.

I thank you Lord for having used me to be a blessing to others. I pray that, sometime in the future, I can also take this message to people who don't know You at all. Everyday I get hungrier to be filled by You so that others can 'eat and drink' from God's Word through me. My desire to someday work full-time for your Kingdom just keeps on growing. People need to know who You are and what You want to mean to them. My heart and my soul are longing to give myself completely to that which You have for me. As much as I enjoy my job at the Child Welfare Council, there is so much more of eternal value out there that I would like to do.

The Pastor of the church where I had given my testimony called to ask if I could do it again the following week during the Dutch service. I agreed and that service was also very beautiful and blessed. That Sunday would also be the last day of my vacation in Curaçao.

Chapter eighteen

∎

But you will receive power when the Holy Spirit has come
upon you, and you will be my witnesses in Jerusalem and in
all Judea and Samaria, and to the end of the earth.
Acts 1:8

Once again it was very hard for me to return to Holland.
This time I had the feeling that, besides my job, I had very
little to return to. I noticed that I had already made a lot of
progress with my emotional healing process and because of
this I had less need for Holland as a place to recover. During
the first days after arriving in Holland I was depressed and
very homesick. Besides that, my 'relationship' with Carl
remained a nagging pain in my life. I never heard from him
again since the talk I had with his Pastor. This made me
realize that as far as Carl was concerned everything was
definitely over. After being back in Holland a few days, I
suddenly fell into a terrible pit of guilt, self pity, bitterness
and resentment. And the pain from abandonment burst out
in me with great intensity.

Tuesday, June 11, 2002

I'm angry at Carl but also at myself because all kinds of feelings and thoughts are coming up inside of me, things that I thought I had already gotten over. Now I'm crying again before the Lord and I feel bad because I threw away and ruined my own marriage. I threw it away, not because I wanted to but because I made so many mistakes I wasn't even aware of. My immature behavior and my insecurity have ruined everything for me. Now it's over and Carl isn't even giving me a second look. He himself admits that he's never done so since he left me. I'm very displeased with him. I think it's mean and unfair of him to walk out on me like he did, but my biggest problem is that he has absolutely no regrets and that he's never ever even given me a chance to make things right again. He doesn't even seem to be asking himself whether or not he has done the right thing by leaving me behind like a dog while he happily continues his life. He left me at the time, he said, because I was too determined to live for the Lord and because of this we were growing apart, but now this same Carl has a girlfriend who is also a Christian and he's more than willing to adapt himself to her Christian lifestyle. Besides, wasn't Carl aware of my faults and shortcomings long before we got married? But he still chose to be with me and marry me, just to leave me behind like old dirt four years later.

I was so downcast that I called my best friend in Curaçao and sent an e-mail to both her and Lucia. My best friend comforted and encouraged me. She reminded me that the Lord was with me and that He had a plan with my life that was so great that I could hardly imagine. Concerning my self condemnation she said that satan was condemning me but that God had forgiven me a long time ago for my mistakes of the past. I was very encouraged when, around midnight, I read and re-read the e-mail she sent me. When I spoke to Lucia on the phone she also said to me: "The Lord has already forgiven you and you have asked Carl for forgiveness, so leave it behind you." Both my best friend and Lucia urged me to accept the Lord's forgiveness and continue with my life. Lucia prayed for me and asked the Lord: "Lord, if Carl is the man for Melanie, do not allow anyone to run off with him, but if You have someone else in mind for her, bring him to her, Lord!" She said that she would continue to pray for me and encouraged me to do the same. In that same conversation she informed me that meanwhile Carl had been baptized.

In spite of the pain I experienced concerning Carl and my divorce, my spiritual growth and my enthusiasm for the Lord continued unabated. I experienced more and more of the anointing of the Holy Spirit in my life and enjoyed the many opportunities I got to tell others about Him.

Sunday, July 07, 2002

Last week I gave my testimony at a Spanish church in Holland. Just like in Curaçao the people were moved. Some of them had been in similar situations and told me that they were strengthened by the Word. Others said that their faith was greatly built up. The great thing about giving my testimony this time was that I myself was allowed to pray with the people after speaking to them. It was beautiful to be able to minister to them in this way. To have been able to do this was true bliss for me. Awesome!

My prayers are powerful again and I'm serving the Lord more consciously every day. I find myself waking up in prayer, worshipping the Lord or doing warfare in the spirit. I can't help but keep picking up my Bible and reading it, hungry for what the Lord has to say to me again. Even in my contacts with colleagues and others that I meet, I notice that His presence is very real to me. Lord, I thank You for this. More than ever I want to live a holy and worthy life before You so that Your power and influence can become even stronger in and through my life.

Friday, July 12, 2002

I'm getting the opportunity very often now to tell my colleagues at work about the Lord. They often come to me, ask me questions and talk to me about the things they have on their mind. One colleague, for example, told me that she has a hard time forgiving her mom. I was able to talk to her about what the Lord expects of us in those type of situations. While I was talking to her she suddenly exclaimed: "Melanie, it seems like the room is getting 'full' while you're talking to me. There is 'something' in the room." I explained to her that what she sensed was the presence of the Lord, the Holy Spirit, and that He was there assisting me while I spoke to her. She could hardly imagine that this was possible, but at the same time she could not deny the reality of what she experienced. Besides talking about forgiveness we also spoke about the joy that the Lord gives. She then told me that she now understands why I am always so exuberant and enjoyed my life so much.

Wednesday, July 17, 2002
After it became known that I chose to work one day less a week at the Child Welfare Council a colleague asked me what I was planning to do with my extra free day. I told him that I wanted to make a start with the writing of my book (yes, this book) and that for the most part it was about my faith in the Lord Jesus. He said that he enjoyed seeing how I daily walked out my faith on the work floor and that he could see that I put my faith into action. He said that he could see that my faith was a lifestyle to me. Next, he asked me to explain to him what the essence of my faith is. I grabbed this opportunity with both hands and told him about Jesus, His death and resurrection, forgiveness of sins, the power of the Word and much more. He listened and asked questions.

This colleague himself does not believe in God but he says that he has learnt to accept that some things in life work out while others don't. I told him that as long as he was still alive, he had the opportunity to give God a try and to call on Him at any moment.

As he was unable to understand everything I said, I let him know that he could say to God: "I call on the God that Melanie told me about." I guaranteed him that the Lord would be right there to help him and to reveal Himself to him. It's so great to be able to talk to others about the Lord in this way, without any kind of pressure. Furthermore, I could tell them about the reality of who Jesus is in my life.

Chapter nineteen

∎

And the ransomed of the LORD shall return and come to
Zion with singing; everlasting joy shall be upon their heads;
they shall obtain gladness and joy, and sorrow and sighing
shall flee away.
Isaiah 35:10

So, this was how I walked with the Lord daily, enjoying
Him more and more each day. I was also excited about what
He was doing in and through my personal life. As promised,
my friends in Curaçao continued praying for me and asking
the Lord to make things clear to me concerning Carl and
myself.

Two months later on September 28, 2002 I was driving to
the city of Etten-Leur with a friend where we had planned a
prayer vigil at another friend's home. That night, we were to
bring our personal needs before the Lord in prayer, call on
Him, and worship Him throughout the night. While we were
on our way I spoke to my friend about my prayer request for
that night: "I'm going to ask the Lord for a miracle so that
Carl and I could be together again. How can it be God's will
for us to be separated?" But not even a minute later I said:
"I don't have any desire to be with Carl anymore, but isn't

it always God's will for a broken marriage to be restored?" Finally, I admitted with a deep sigh that I really didn't know what to ask God for concerning my relationship with Carl. My friend listened to me patiently and then suggested that we ask God during the prayer vigil to make His will known in this situation. So, that was what we did. After we reached Etten-Leur and had spent several hours in prayer and worshipping the Lord, my long awaited breakthrough finally came!

Saturday, September 28, 2002
Out of the blue in this night the moment came in which a word of the Holy Spirit spoken by a friend of mine pierced right through me, when she said: "Melanie, do you know that you are struggling with a spirit of rejection?" I looked at her and thought: "Yes, I know that I was rejected when I was young and that as a consequence of this I had an inferiority complex. I also know now that this has seeped into my marriage and that it ultimately made Carl not want to continue his life with me anymore." But it was not until that moment that it really got across to me that this spirit of rejection was also the reason why I was unable to let Carl go, even when I really didn't have a problem with the fact that he no longer wanted to be with me.
All of a sudden it all became clear to me: my continual struggle and 'desire' to be reunited with Carl had nothing at all to do with love for him anymore. My obsession for

restoration didn't come forth out of love, but it came out of a need that was still hidden deep down inside of me. The little girl in me needed to hear from the one who had rejected her that she was still worthwhile. I still longed for recognition and acceptance from Carl. It was not that I wanted to have Carl back in my life. It was not that I wanted restoration, but I needed to know that in Carl's eyes I was still good enough and deserved a second chance, even if I had no intention at all to make use of a possible second chance.

The Lord had already shown me in a very early stage what was the background of my mistakes made in my marriage. He healed me of them and forgave me, but there was still more to be done. Up until tonight the past was still a hindrance for me and made me unable to build up my life in a positive way and cut myself loose from Carl. But since the prayer vigil something changed inside of me. I became free! It is also only now that I'm able to completely forgive myself for my mistakes and shortcomings in my marriage. The yoke has been broken! Lord, you are so good to me! I praise Your name for what You have done in my life this night!

On that night in Etten-Leur that dominating force of rejection and feelings of inferiority were broken off my life through a word of knowledge and warfare-like prayer of all those present. From that moment on I was able to put Carl and my broken marriage behind me for once and for all. That awesome night was the last time that Carl played a role of any significance in my life.

Lord, I didn't understand before that this was the path that You had for me to travel on: Carl's salvation and my complete inner and spiritual healing. Looking back, I'm grateful to You that I had this experience. Even though this has been the most difficult time in my life up till now, it was also the most beautiful and most valuable. I have a deep love and respect for You and your tender dealings in my life. You have been my husband, my best friend, my joy, my support and my refuge. I have learned that real joy in my life only comes from knowing and recognizing You as the source of everything I will ever need or desire. No person or circumstance can fulfill me as You have proven that only You are able to do. My life is richly filled in You and with You.

Even though I would someday like to have a relationship again, it's no longer a prerequisite to a happy life. A partner and husband may enrich my life, but will never fulfill it: for this, You have already done!

The last I heard about Carl was that he was an active youth leader in his church and that he had started a prayer group at his office. By bringing this to my attention the Lord showed me that all my prayers for Carl had been answered: He had given his life to the Lord, was baptized, became a preacher of God's Word and had grown to love the Lord!

Sunday, December 15, 2002 was the last time I wrote in my diary. Looking back, it seems that from the very beginning it was God's intention for me to preserve my story plainly and clearly, my story that hopefully will serve as a testimony for many people. The last entry made in my diary describes a word that I received from a sister from the church I attended. This word confirmed and was a reminder of the words spoken over my life on June 4, 2000 by my Pastor in Curaçao and on October 27, 2001 at the 'Day of Refreshing'.

Sunday, December 15, 2002
She saw a vision of a farm where bread was being baked and distributed to the people, and said: "The Lord is going to use you to share His word with others in love, with authority and with fire. Those who hear you speak will recognize and know that you have reason to speak about Jesus. Be bold and courageous." Without knowing about my personal situation she also spoke the following words: "I am seeing an image of two rings surrounded by lovely, white flowers. The Lord is reminding you that He has a covenant with you and that He will always be faithful to you. The symbol of the rings also speaks of purity, restoration and new things." This is the word I received today. And I remember that it was just yesterday that I asked the Lord: "Lord, will I ever get married again?"

While the sister spoke these words that morning, in my heart, I felt that the image of the rings had a double meaning for me.

Chapter twenty

■

Blessed is the man who remains steadfast under trial, for when he has stood the test he will receive the crown of life, which God has promised to those who love him.
James 1:12

I will greatly rejoice in the LORD; my soul shall exult in my God, for he has clothed me with the garments of salvation; he has covered me with the robe of righteousness, as a bridegroom decks himself like a priest with a beautiful headdress, and as a bride adorns herself with her jewels.
Isaiah 61:10

Weeks and months went by and I noticed that the chapter 'Carl' was definitely closed in my life. I didn't think of him any more and no longer reverted to thinking whether or not he and I would ever make amends. A load had fallen off my shoulders and I was finally free!! Made free indeed by the Lord (John 8:36). I was free to look forward to the future as a new person and focus on all that the Lord still had in store for me!

In the next three chapters I will describe the events that took place after my deliverance and after the word I received in December 2002.

One day in November 2002, I met a friend of mine whom I had not seen in a long time. She told me that she met a nice man through a Christian dating site. I was happy for her but told her that I really didn't think that that was an appropriate way to meet someone. Through the internet?!

It was a few months later, in January 2003, that I began having the desire to start a new relationship. I started praying about this very earnestly and asked the Lord for certain very specific character traits that I wanted to see in my future husband. I prayed for a man who loved the Lord and had a desire to serve Him. Not a perfect man, but one with a special heart for his fellowmen who was out to share the love of Christ with others. I also prayed: "Lord, if it's to be a Dutchman let him be acquainted and feel comfortable with people of other cultures. During one of my prayer times I even prayed the following: "Lord, give me a man who is divorced, just like I am, but let it be so that it is not he who walked out on his wife, but that his wife walked out on him." I couldn't understand why I would ask the Lord for something like this, but I did.

After a few weeks my prayer changed from prayerfully asking, to a proclamation. Again a few weeks later there was a certainty, deep in my heart, that the Lord had heard my prayers. I began thanking him with joy for what was coming my way, my heart full of peace and conviction.

It was around this same time that I felt that it was time to leave Holland and return to the warmth of my birth island

and my family and friends. So, I was very busy making preparations for my trip back home. But all my Christian friends warned me that, in their opinion, I was making an emotional decision. They didn't think it was my 'time' yet to return to Curaçao. In spite of all the warnings, I persistently continued with my plans. I gave up my job at the Child Welfare Council, booked a ticket to Curaçao and was scheduled to leave on May 29th 2003.

Yet, between my decision to leave Holland and my definite departure there were some incidents that took place one after another that made me begin to doubt whether I had really made the right decision. One of the things that happened was that the clerk of the housing association was not able to find any 'termination of tenancy'-forms at the office when I went to terminate my contract for the apartment. She was very embarrassed as she apologized for this and told me that she would send a form to my home address as soon as possible. Also, my visit to the town hall was in vain. The municipal worker said to me: "Miss, it's not a good idea to do that right now. You will be better off waiting until about five days before your definite departure to have your name removed from the municipal register. So, on that day all doors were closed for me.

One month before I planned to leave Holland on April 24th, 2003 I was leafing through a Christian magazine that I had received by mail. I found out later that the same friend who had taken me to the prayer vigil in Etten-Leur had arranged a trial subscription for me. All of a sudden my eyes were caught by an advertisement for the Christian dating site that my friend had told me about five months earlier. I recognized the name of the site and decided to log in out of pure curiosity. It was a matter of minutes before a profile of a 32 year old Dutchman, Richard, from the city of Almere caught my attention. He wrote that he would like to meet a Christian woman with whom he could share his life and told about the pain of his divorce after his ex-wife had suddenly left him for another man, after almost six years of marriage. This blow came a few months after he had decided to dedicate his life completely to the Lord. Richard told of how he had experienced the Lord as never before during this difficult period. God proved himself to him to be a faithful and loving Father who carried him through his pain. The honesty of his words appealed to me so much, that I immediately sent him a short e-mail. I also wrote about my plans to move to Curaçao one month later.

In the four days that followed there was intensive e-mail contact between Eindhoven and Almere. There were also some telephone conversations. Richard e-mailed me that he was happy for me that I was able to make the trip back to my island. With reference to this he let me know that he himself had many friends from Surinam and Turkish descent. He also wrote that, for some time now, he had the desire to move to a foreign country some day in the future. While reading his e-mails I realized with astonishment that

147

he was telling me things that I had specifically asked God for in prayer some months before.

Richard also told me how he ended up on the dating site. After his wife had left him there was a short period in which he turned his back on God and went back to the world. He did this in an effort to regain his self confidence. He had the need to be affirmed and needed to know that he was still 'in demand', considering that his self image had gotten a terrible blow. Even though there were enough women who showed interest in him, Richard soon had to admit that this lifestyle brought him no inner peace and joy. Besides, the women he met while going out didn't want to have anything at all to do with the Lord.

But Richard wanted to pick up his life again and meet a new life partner so he registered at the Christian dating site. However, more than once the thought entered his mind: "Isn't this way of seeking contact only for desperate people? What am I doing here?" But within a few weeks he got so many positive reactions that he slowly began regaining his self confidence. Still, the dates he went on made him uneasy and even gave him an uncomfortable feeling. Right before I reacted on his profile Richard had just decided to leave the dating site for what it was and find his peace in the Lord once again. He began praying and asked the Lord to send him a woman who loved the Lord so that they could serve Him together. During a prayer meeting in March 2003 at his home church in Amsterdam, a Surinam friend of Richard prayed for him that he would meet his new wife soon. This friend, who had given his life to the Lord not long before, felt deep in his spirit that the Lord had heard his prayer for his friend Richard, but he couldn't explain why he was so sure of this.

It was after this prayer that Richard decided to take one last look on the dating site and found my e-mail of April 24, 2003.

Chapter twenty one

∎

My beloved speaks and says to me: "Arise, my love, my beautiful one, and come away, for behold, the winter is past; the rain is over and gone. The flowers appear on the earth, the time of singing has come, and the voice of the turtledove is heard in our land.
Song of Solomon 2:10-12

Without really knowing who Richard was I felt very much at ease with him during our telephone conversations. Besides, as far as I could see he seemed to have practically all the characteristics that I had so specifically asked the Lord for. In the meantime, Richard was also convinced that his contact with me was different to the others he had. Finally our curiosity got the better of us and we arranged to meet in Eindhoven on April 29th, 2003. Before going to sleep I deliberated with the Lord what all this could mean, and that night I had a dream: I dreamed that I was sitting in a car on the passenger side. I couldn't see that there was anyone sitting next to me, but I did hear Richards voice which I had heard many times over the phone by now, saying: "I'm going to call the women that I met on the dating site to let them know that I found the woman I want to continue my life with." The next morning I was laughing when I told the dream to a friend of mine who was spending the night at my house.

The next evening I was nervous and excited as I got ready for my first date with Richard. My friend and I had been very busy picking out my nicest clothes for this evening. I spent a lot of time on my hair, but in the end still was not satisfied with the result. Finally, I was ready and I sat nervously waiting for Richard, while talking to my friend as she tried to finish a homework-assignment on the computer. I jumped up when the door bell rang. My heart was pounding and beating wildly. On the other side of the intercom the now familiar sound of Richard's voice announced his arrival. A few more seconds and he would be upstairs. I ran to the bedroom one last time and quickly checked myself in the mirror. I walked back to the hall, opened the door and there he stood: a little shorter than I initially expected but for the rest, not at all bad. He had a boyish and athletic appearance and just like in our telephone conversations, he was open and spontaneous.

Richard sat on the couch for a while as we talked nervously with each other. Soon after that we decided to head for downtown Eindhoven. Sitting in the car I had all the time to have a good look at Richard while chatting with him. Well, well, well what a nice guy: twinkling little eyes and a friendly smile when he spoke. I also noticed his nice hands while he drove (for some reason I pay a lot of attention to this). It all looked very good and the ride to the city was very pleasant as well.

Once we reached town there was a large crowd gathered there in connection with the festivities on the eve before the celebration of the Queen's birthday. There was loud music playing everywhere and there were many drunk people walking around, singing loudly or trying their best to be funny. We went into one of the first cafes we met at the outskirts of the city. It was so crowded that we ended up having to share a table with some other people. Richard and I sat next to each other but there was so much noise around us that it was hard for us to understand each other when we talked. We practically had to shout into each other's ears to have somewhat of a conversation. Still, it soon became obvious that there was a 'click' between us. We had more than enough to talk about.

After I finished drinking my ice-tea and Richard his beer, we decided to look for a more quiet place. We first had to make our way through the large crowd but then finally got to a quiet cafe on the other side of town. Besides us, there were only two other people sitting at a table next to the window. We headed for a table all the way at the back of the café and ordered something to drink. This time Richard and I sat opposite of each other. At least here we were able to talk in a tranquil environment.

Richard told me that he wanted to get on with his life. Yet it was soon apparent that he was not yet completely healed from the pain of his divorce and everything surrounding it. From my own experience I knew that this could be a long and tiresome process and we spoke about this at length. The atmosphere was calm and relaxed while we spoke about many different things.

I noticed that I was very nervous as I spoke to Richard. I felt butterflies in my stomach and more than once during our date I ran to the restroom to recollect myself and say a little prayer: "Lord, I like him, I really like him, but Lord, what does he think about me? I don't have a clue what he thinks about me and what about his ex wife, Lord?"

After spending a pleasant evening together it was time to return home. Richard still had to make the long drive back all the way to Almere after dropping me off at my apartment in Eindhoven. Great was my surprise, when we said our goodbyes sitting in the car and Richard said to me: "I'm going to call the women that I met on the dating site to let them know that I found the woman I want to continue my life with." Oh Lord, I thought, is this really possible? Richard had repeated the exact words that I heard in my dream the night before. From that moment on I knew for sure: this was a confirmation of God Almighty that Richard would be my future husband! Since that day Richard and I spent as much time as we could together, either in Almere or in Eindhoven.

Chapter twenty two

■

But thanks be to God, who gives us the victory through our
Lord Jesus Christ.
1 Corinthians 15:5

Besides good times there were also difficult periods
and tough conversations in the first few months with
Richard, concerning his former relationship. Richard was
sure that he wanted to build up a relationship with me, but
he sometimes still struggled with the thought whether or
not the Lord expected him to leave an open door in case his
ex-wife would change her mind and return to him. I on my
part often cried before the Lord and called my best friend
on the phone saying that I didn't want to become attached to
Richard and run the risk of suddenly losing him again.

One day in July of 2003 I had a strong urge again to
write and get things off my chest. I was at work, a job that
I got through the employment agency at the Department
for Youth Welfare, after I had given up my job at the Child
Welfare Council. I didn't have my diary with me so I jotted
down my frustrations on a piece of paper. My writing was
directed both to the Lord and to Richard and consisted of
the following:

Lord, what is the meaning of this? Where is this heading? I thought that everything was going so well and didn't even consider that things could still go wrong. I feel heavy and sick in my heart. Why? Why does it seem as if I'm not allowed to be happy? Lord, why doesn't Richard know what he wants? Why did we meet each other then, if things have to go like this? I prayed for him, for a man like him. You wouldn't give me what I ask for if it isn't good for me, would you Lord?! I'm still convinced that he is the one you have for me. I want Richard to find his rest in You. Give him a wink, Lord. He needs You so badly. Allow his heart to find your 'Father heart' and lead him into his destiny. He loves you, Lord, but his struggle is long and difficult. Know his heart, Lord, and reward him according to his heart's condition.

Finally I wrote:

Richard, I'm praying for you that your life path will be so clear and so beautiful as you have never imagined possible. I'm praying for you. I love you.

      The struggles we went through made Richard and I grow closer to God and to each other. We had no choice but to keep going back to the Lord in prayer. We prayed and begged Him to reveal and confirm to us what it was that He wanted for both of us. And as the Lord was accustomed

155

doing in my life and according to the promise of his Word, this situation was also solved after some weeks of fervent prayer.

In the month of August 2003 there was a guest speaker from the United States visiting our church. Richard received the sermon he gave as a confirmation that it was okay for him to leave his past and his former marriage behind him.

And two days later the Lord confirmed this with an unmistakable experience: Richard and I had a sudden encounter with his ex-wife and her new boyfriend, while shopping in the city of Almere. We stood eye to eye with each other leaving us no choice but to introduce ourselves and have a short chat. After a few minutes of meaningless chatter we went our way again. After this meeting Richard said to me: "We are like strangers to each other. I can hardly imagine that I was ever married to her. There's nothing left between us." From that moment on Richard and I both knew, without any doubt, that this encounter was a last answer to our prayers. Right after that Richard was able to completely let go of his ex-wife and his former marriage.

Looking back, I compare this period with the story in the Old Testament of the Bible in which God gave the Israelites the promise of entering the Promised Land. The promise was there but entering that land would not go without a battle. They had to fight and face adversities to get there, but get there they would! God himself would make sure of that! In my heart I knew for sure that God had given me and Richard to each other but still there were hurdles for us to overcome. The fact that my prayer for a husband was answered did not mean that I wouldn't have to face struggles, but the victory was already there for me, even though I was unable to see it from the beginning.

After bumping into Richard's ex-wife we were able to completely focus ourselves on our plans for the future. Our relationship grew closer and deeper everyday and we were married only 10 months after we met, on February 12th, 2004. The wedding day was filled with joy and love.

In the past I have often asked myself if I would ever meet someone again who would love me as much as Carl did, or who I could love as much. Now, after being married for two years I realize that the Lord has outdone Himself in this area also! Richard and I have both prayed fervently and have struggled in vain to maintain our former marriage, but the grace of God ultimately proved to us that He was able to turn a difficult, painful experience into blessing and joy. I received a new life-partner from the Lord, a relationship that was born out of prayer, contrary to the former one. And prayer, as I learned now, should be the most important basis for every decision in a person's life. I can't say that we have a fairytale marriage, even though I do experience it like that at times, but we do have a pleasant and very blessed marriage relationship. The Lord gave me a husband whom I can complement and be an enrichment to, just as he is for me. Of course we both need to continue working on our marriage relationship just like any other couple, without ever taking what we have for granted.

By the mercy of God I realize daily that I am changed for the better: I no longer try to derive my self-esteem from my husband, I'm learning to communicate better each day and I'm no longer afraid to speak up about those things that bother me or work on my nerves. Besides that, Richard and I have made it a habit to go to the Lord in prayer together, especially when we have disagreements, asking Him to help us and give us wisdom to deal with our own faults and shortcomings. Our joint relationship with God makes it possible for our marriage to remain solid. We both realize that the condition for a strong and lasting marriage is for us to always remain close to the Lord, and in this we each have our own personal responsibility.

Since I met Richard we've been to Curaçao on vacation four times and we always had a great time with my family and friends. From the first time Richard visited the island he felt very much at home there and with the people he met.

During and after the first three vacations we sometimes considered moving permanently to Curaçao.

However, this desire never lasted very long and we still had many doubts about our plans. Usually our desire completely faded away within a few weeks of returning to Holland. But the fourth vacation from December 28th, 2005 to January 18th, 2006 was different.

First of all two pregnancy tests during that great vacation confirmed that we were pregnant of our first child. Secondly, we experienced some very special times with a couple working as missionaries on the island. They are actively involved in the ministry among prisoners in Curaçao. Mainly due to them, our eyes were opened to the many possibilities to be of service to the Curaçao community, for example under the less fortunate youth and teenage mothers. We were enthusiastic and brought our growing desire to be of service in Curaçao, in prayer before the Lord daily. Toward the end of the vacation we were both convinced that a move to Curaçao was going to be the next step that we were allowed to make in our life. The desire to do so had never before been so constant and so definite during any of our former vacations.

The day before returning to Holland Richard went for a job interview at a company he had visited a year earlier. After reaching back in Holland he got a call from them saying that they would like to offer him a job. From that point on the Lord "arranged" everything we needed to be able to make the transfer to Curaçao in a quick pace: Richard's brother would rent our house in Holland (which we didn't want to sell). We found a buyer for our car, we found a suitable home to rent in Curaçao and the company that hired Richard offered us an attractive compensation to ship our furniture to Curaçao. So, this was the way that the necessary steps were made, supported by much prayer, for our move to Curaçao. Our date of departure was planned for May 20th, 2006.

And so the circle was made complete. Three years ago I was planning to return to Curaçao on May 29, 2003, all alone, but the Lord had other plans. He still had blessings stored away for me. Blessings that I would not have wanted to miss out on. And now, exactly three years later in May of 2006, I'm returning to my beloved island but richly blessed: I have my husband at my side and a baby on the way. Lord, truly Your mercy is great!! Richard and I are enthusiastic and look forward to this new and exciting phase in our lives. One thing we know for sure: we can trust the Lord to continue guiding us in the same way He has done during the past few years!

Lord, we put our trust in You and thank You in advance for a blessed and meaningful time in Curaçao. We also thank You that we can look forward to a fantastic future with You!

Epilogue

■

Life takes us through many unexpected and unpleasant moments which we just find ourselves having to deal with. Sometimes we hope for a certain outcome, but things tend to turn out completely different than we expect. We will never understand everything that takes place in our lives. For example, concerning my situation God says in His Word: "I hate divorce". Nevertheless He allowed this to happen to me. Maybe in your situation you prayed for your sick child, yet death was inevitable. Maybe you suddenly lost a dear friend or family member. You may be depressed or very sick and life looks really gloomy. Or: have you been the victim of rape, incest or abuse? Has your husband or wife been unfaithful to you or did you suddenly lose your job? How is all this possible? Where is God in moments like these and is He really that faithful to His word?

God never promised that life on earth would be a bed of roses, but He did promise that we could count on His support if we trust and include Him in our situation. Unfortunately, total surrender to God is often a tiresome and painful process which we often put off, all because we think that we can make it on our own. Experience shows that, very often, people only really begin seeking God while experiencing pain and troubles. It is therefore only at this time that God can reveal Himself as being very trustworthy and the One who makes the impossible possible in our lives.

In Matthew 7:9-11 Jesus says: : *"Which of you, if his son asks for bread, will give him a stone? Or if he asks for a fish, will give him a snake? If you, then, though you are evil, know how to give good gifts to your children, how much more will your Father in heaven give good gifts to those who ask Him!"* Jesus did not say that the son gets bread when he asks for bread, but he explains that the son will not get a stone. In other words, the son will not get something that is bad for him. But the word of God continues to say that God gives 'good gifts' to those who pray and ask Him for this.

For a long time I had a wrong concept about what 'good gifts' really meant. I thought it must mean that God would answer my prayers exactly the way I asked Him to. But my personal life experience showed me that the good gifts that God gives is Himself. And who is God? He is a Husband to the widow or the abandoned wife, a Healer to the sick, Joy to the one who is sad. In other words 'good gifts' is God Himself and all that He has destined for us to be able to cope with life's difficulties, no matter what comes our way. And if for whatever reason God chooses not to heal, not to restore, or not to deliver, we must still continue believing that He knows what's best and therefore we must continue to reach out to Him. Because, who else can we really turn to for help? Who else can carry us through the difficult times of life and both strengthen and transform us?

I believe that we all have a choice to make not to stand still at the 'deep valleys' of life, but to give God the opportunity to prove to us that life doesn't end with that one valley. God is infinitely great and has an infinite amount of beautiful and worthwhile experiences stored up for us, if only we dare to look further. We must take hold of these blessings and not allow them to pass us by.

The Lord has changed me throughout this whole process. He allowed someone to be taken away from me who was very precious to me, that one person of which I thought I would cease to exist if he would ever be taken away from me. But in doing this God has taught me that He alone could give me what no human being or situation could ever give me. I certainly do not want to create the impression that we will always easily and effortlessly conquer all problems that we encounter on our life path with God on our side. No one will ever ask to go through pain and difficulty, but I want to share this with you: it has given me strength and courage to have learned that God alone is sufficient for me!

Conclusion

.

After reading this book you might think: I don't know God but I also want to build up a relationship with Him and learn to trust Him in every area of my life. I too want to reach a point in my life where I can say that, whatever happens, my relationship with God and my faith in Him are the most important things. Maybe you knew the Lord but you turned your back on Him because of disappointments or because you didn't think that He was there for you as He should have been. It's also possible that you as a believer or unbeliever reading this book are going through a difficult time. You may be asking yourself: "How in the world will I get through this?" I want to encourage you to include the Lord in your situation. His way may not be the one you had imagined for yourself, but you can trust that He wants the best for you. Just put your trust in Him.

The first step to an intimate relationship with God as described in this book is to use the Bible as the absolute guiding principle for your life and to believe in God's son Jesus Christ. If you have a hard time accepting these two facts then, please, ask God to help you understand why these are so important. The Bible teaches us that Jesus died for us on the cross more than 2000 years ago and that He is the only way to get to God, the Father (John 14:6).

We can have a relationship with the invisible God when we understand who Jesus is (John 14:9). Jesus walked the earth and demonstrated the character traits of the invisible God, His Father who is: the Deliverer, Healer, Provider, a Worker of miracles, the Loving and Forgiving One. He shows compassion for the pain we go through and carries us through difficult times, if only we would allow Him to. But God is also holy and righteous and therefore tough in His dealings with sin and hypocrisy. The Bible also says that Jesus is the same yesterday, today and forever more (Hebrews 13:8). This means that He is still able to do the things He did 2000 years ago. Yet, in order for us to see this manifest in our life, we need to believe in Him.

Faith in Jesus Christ gives us a desire to live for God and also enables us to actually do so. This same faith also gives us the peace and security of knowing that we have eternal life with God, when our life here on earth comes to an end. After making a choice to believe in Jesus Christ, life will not always be easy, but you can know for sure that God will carry you through every situation when you ask Him to. You may also know for certain that you can claim every promise that is written in the Bible, for yourself.

If you want to take this step of faith I would first like to encourage you to browse through one of the four gospels (the books of Matthew, Mark, Luke and John) in the Bible. Particularly the book of John gives a clear understanding of who Jesus is and what the reason was for His coming to this world. It also tells of all the things He did while He walked the earth. If you would like to make Jesus part of your life or if you want to re-dedicate your life to Him you can pray the following prayer:

Lord Jesus, I believe in You. I believe that You are the Son of God and that You died for my sins, just as it is written in the Bible. I'm sorry for all the things I did in my life that hurt You. Forgive me of my sins, come into my life, take control of my life and make me the way You want me to be. With Your help I renounce all my sinful deeds and ways of the past. From this day forth I want to confess You as my Lord and my Savior. Thank you Lord. In Jesus' name.

If you have prayed the above prayer with a sincere heart, the Bible says that you have now been given the right to become a child of God (John 1:12). This means that from this moment on you are equipped to truly be able to live as a child of God, a life that is pleasing to Him and to enjoy his blessings. You do this by appropriating the Word of God and applying it to your life, knowing that all the promises and blessings in the Bible are for you. You may claim them as words that God is speaking directly to you. The following list is a small selection from the hundreds of promises and blessings in the Bible:

- *The LORD is close to the brokenhearted and saves those*

who are crushed in spirit. (Psalms 34:18)

- *Call to me and I will answer you and tell you great and unsearchable things you do not know. (Jeremiah 33:3)*
- *Then you will know that I am the LORD; those who hope in me will not be disappointed. (Isaiah 49:23)*
- *For the eyes of the LORD range throughout the earth to strengthen those whose hearts are fully committed to him. (2 Chronicles 16:9)*
- *Delight yourself in the LORD and he will give you the desires of your heart. (Psalms 37:4)*
- *If we confess our sins, he is faithful and just and will forgive us our sins and purify us from all unrighteousness. (1 John 1:9)*
- *Therefore, if anyone is in Christ, he is a new creation; the old has gone, the new has come! (2 Corinthians 5:17)*
- *Cast all your anxiety on him because he cares for you. (1 Peter 5:7)*

The Lord expects us to obey Him. Continuing to go our own way or refusing to take account of God could be a hindrance for God answering our prayers. Some examples of this could be seen in the following Bible verses:

- *Dear friends, if our hearts do not condemn us, we have confidence before God and receive from him anything we ask, because we obey his commands and do what pleases him. (1 John 3:21-22)*

- *if my people, who are called by my name, will humble themselves and pray and seek my face and turn from their wicked ways, then will I hear from heaven and will forgive their sin and will heal their land. (2 Chronicles 7:14)*

- *Obey me, and I will be your God and you will be my people. Walk in all the ways I command you, that it may go well with you. (Jeremiah 7:23)*

I want to further encourage you to:

1. Talk to God daily (pray) about everything you go through during your day. Talk to Him about the things you desire for yourself and others. After you pray take the time to wait in silence for a while, God may give you the solutions and answers to your petitions right then and there. Also, be sure to immediately ask the Lord for forgiveness if you say or do something wrong. This way you prevent sin from separating you from God's nearness.

2. Read the Bible every day so that God Himself can speak to you, encourage you and/or exhort you. Many things in the Bible may be difficult for you to understand at first. It may also be difficult to read from God's word on a regular basis. You may also totally disagree with some of the things you read. If need be, skip those parts that do not immediately appeal to you. I want to

encourage you: Please do not just reject the whole Bible on account of this, but continue reading it. In doing so you will soon begin to gain more understanding of it and you will even find yourself developing a love for God's Word when you learn to apply it in your daily life and notice the great power that flows from its pages.

3. Seek a church community where the Word of God is preached and where you can worship the Lord with other believers and be an encouragement for one another. Here I want to give a marginal note: even in church there are going to be people who will disappoint you. We as children of God are all on a journey that is meant to bring us closer to God, but as long as we're still living on this earth we will make mistakes and have our shortcomings. We will only achieve perfection when we are forever (re)united with our God in heaven. Besides, when Jesus walked on this earth, He said: "Follow me". (John 1:44 and 21:23). So, we're not called to follow other people, but we're called to follow Jesus and do that which He asks of us.

Finally, I want to refer you to the Internet sites www. christiananswers.net and www.jesusmessiah.com where you can become further acquainted with God in many of His facets. I pray that the rest of your life may be filled with all the 'good gifts' that God has for you!

The LORD will call you back
as if you were a wife deserted and distressed in
spirit—
a wife who married young,
only to be rejected," says your God.

"For a brief moment I abandoned you,
but with deep compassion I will bring you back.
In a surge of anger
I hid my face from you for a moment,
but with everlasting kindness
I will have compassion on you,"
says the LORD your Redeemer.
"To me this is like the days of Noah,
when I swore that the waters of Noah would never
again cover the earth.
So now I have sworn not to be angry with you,
never to rebuke you again.
Though the mountains be shaken
and the hills be removed,
yet my unfailing love for you will not be shaken
nor my covenant of peace be removed,"
says the LORD, who has compassion on you.
(Isaiah 54:6-10)

About the author

■

The author Melanie Kos-Paula was born in Curaçao in 1969. At the age of 18 she moved to the United States where she majored in 'Human Development' and earned her Bachelors Degree. Beginning 1991 she fulfilled several functions in Curaçao as well as in Holland, among other things giving 'social skills' training to the youth and female (ex) prisoners and providing aid for refugees. She also offered counseling and courses for parents, teachers and children in an effort to help restore disrupted relationships between them. From 2001 to 2006 she had an advisory function with the department of criminal affairs of the Child Welfare Council in Holland, first in Eindhoven and later in Lelystad.

Although she was actively involved with the Pentecostal Church at a very early age, it was not until 1999 that her spiritual life really gained meaning and she began to understand how she could make God an active partner in her day to day life.

In May of 2006 she returned to her island of birth with her family. It is her desire to be able to share with others her experiences as described in this book and allow them to learn about the many things that God is able to do in their lives.

Notes

.

Chapter 2

1.   Catherine Marshall, The Helper,
      (Chosen Books Publishing Co., 1978)
2.   Benny Hinn, Good Morning, Holy Spirit
      (Thomas Nelson Publishers, 1990, 1997)

Chapter 3

1.   A.J. Russel, Two Listeners, God Calling
      (Barbour Publishing, Incorporated)

Chapter 4

1.   Darien. B. Cooper, You can be the Wife of a Happy
      Husband (Chariot Victor Publishing, 1977)
2.   Gary Chapman, The Five Love Languages
      (Northfield Publishing, 1992, 1995)

Chapter 5

1.   The Amplified Bible
      (Zondervan Publishing House, 1987)

Chapter 11

1.   Robert T. Boyd, World's Bible Handbook
      (World Publishing, 1991)

Chapter 14

1.   Andrew Murray, The Ministry of Intercession
      (Whitaker House, 1982)

www.ingramcontent.com/pod-product-compliance
Lightning Source LLC
LaVergne TN
LVHW011420080426
835512LV00005B/161